The Fabric of Early Christianity

Helmut and Gisela Koester
on their 50th wedding anniversary

The Fabric of Early Christianity

Reflections in Honor of Helmut Koester
by Fifty Years of Harvard Students
Presented on the Occasion of His 80th Birthday

Edited by
James D. Smith III and Philip Sellew

Pickwick *Publications*

An imprint of *Wipf and Stock Publishers*
199 West 8th Avenue • Eugene OR 97401

THE FABRIC OF EARLY CHRISTIANITY
Reflections in Honor of Helmut Koester by Fifty Years of Harvard Students
Presented on the Occasion of His 80th Birthday

ISBN 10: 1-59752-974-5
ISBN 13: 978-1-49824-875-4

Cataloging-in-publication data

The fabric of early christianity: reflections in honor of Helmut Koester by fifty years of Harvard students presented on the occasion of his 80th birthday / edited by James D. Smith III and Philip Sellew.

xvi + 152 p., 23 cm.

Eugene, Ore.: Pickwick Publications

ISBN 10: 1-59752-974-5
ISBN 13: 978-1-49824-875-4

1. Koester, Helmut, 1926-. 2. Festschriften. 3. Bible. N.T. I. Title.

BR166 F86 2007

Dedicated to three women of Spirit

Gisela Harrassowitz Koester
Kathleen Troxell Sellew
Linda Kathleen Westmoreland Smith

From our youth, through the Harvard years, to this present moment

Faithful and true friends
Beloved lifelong partners
Heirs together of God's grace

Contents

Preface by Philip Sellew and James D. Smith III / ix
Foreword by Krister Stendahl / xiii

The Fifties and Sixties

Everett Ferguson / 1
Eldon Jay Epp / 3
Robert A. Kraft / 9
Arthur Bellinzoni / 12
Norman Petersen / 16
George W. E. Nickelsburg / 19
Birger A. Pearson / 21
Elaine Pagels / 25

The Sixties and Seventies

Archbishop Demetrios (Trakatellis) / 29
David M. Scholer / 32
David L. Tiede / 35
Harold W. Attridge / 40
Richard I. Pervo / 42
Dennis MacDonald / 44
Carolyn Osiek / 46
Dennis E. Smith / 49

The Seventies and Eighties

John J. Clabeaux / 55
Robert F. Stoops, Jr. / 59
Gary A. Bisbee / 62
Philip Sellew / 64
James D. Smith III / 69
Michael O'Laughlin / 73

Stephen J. Patterson / 78
Lee I. McDonald / 83
Daniel Schowalter / 87
Christopher R. Matthews / 90
Steven J. Friesen / 94

The Eighties, Nineties, and Beyond
James C. Walters / 99
Christine M. Thomas / 103
Jennifer Berenson Maclean / 107
Ellen Bradshaw Aitken / 110
Shelly Matthews / 114
Demetrius K. Williams / 118
Ann Graham Brock / 122
Laura Nasrallah / 126
Melanie Johnson-Debaufre / 131
AnneMarie Luijendijk / 136

Afterword by Klaus Baltzer / 139
Notes on Contributors / 145

Preface

WE OFFER this volume of reflections in honor of our teacher Helmut Koester, as this year he celebrates his eightieth birthday and approaches his fiftieth year of teaching at Harvard University in his 'emeritus' role as Morison Research Professor of New Testament Studies and Winn Research Professor of Church History. Fifteen years ago a more traditional Festschrift appeared, *The Future of Early Christianity* (Minneapolis: Fortress Press, 1991). Edited by Birger Pearson, this was an expansive and richly detailed collection of scholarly pieces suggesting the range of Helmut's own interests in the field, and the respect for his work within the larger academic community. In 1998 a special issue of the *Harvard Theological Review* published papers from a symposium assessing the influences and directions of his scholarship on Jesus and the gospel traditions, a moment that might have marked Professor Koester's retirement from the University faculty were it not for the enduring energy and commitment testified to by the tributes to follow.

This volume is of a different genre. It is essentially a collection of *encomia*, reflections by a half-century of Harvard students on Helmut's contribution to our understanding of the New Testament and early Christianity—and his unique contributions to their own lives and thought, research and ministries. Our tributes begin and conclude with reflections from two of Helmut's earliest colleagues and collaborators. Krister Stendahl (already a professor at HDS a few years before Helmut's arrival at the New York Pier described below) offers a characteristically gracious and vivid sketch as our Foreword, while Klaus Baltzer of Munich provides as our Afterword some fascinating comments about his long association with Helmut dating back to their days as young apprentice faculty at the University of Heidelberg and extending through the storied archaeology seminars traveling through Greece and Turkey.

The essays are brief by design; we include no footnotes or bibliography. The contributions are intended not to present the latest research or (re)position an ongoing issue, but to reflect a community of scholars recalling Cambridge days, assessing the intervening years with a minimum of technical apparatus, and joined in expressing personal appreciation for a valued teacher. We believe that, given a strict word limit, each one has effectively placed a colorful tile in the mosaic, has brought a unique strand to be woven into the larger fabric. Among our contributors are a Greek Orthodox Archbishop, a former Bishop of Stockholm, three seminary presidents and three deans of divinity schools, and both the current and several past presidents of the Society of Biblical Literature. Given that these are Koester's students it seems likely that several future SBL presidents lurk within these pages as well.

The process of contacting these fellow Harvard students across the decades, and receiving these essays for review, has been both fulfilling and fun. Jim Smith proposed the idea to Phil Sellew of some sort of tribute during a phone call early in 2006. As our thinking developed, the idea emerged of presenting these tributes in book form during an appropriate session of the SBL meeting in Washington the month before Helmut's eightieth birthday. This goal of course called for a very quick response from our prospective contributors, and we are gratified how many colleagues have risen to the occasion so well. Our heartfelt thanks to each and every one of them for their gracious and timely response. We also thank Dr. Beth Kautz of the University of Minnesota, Helmut's daughter-in-law, for looking over our translation of Professor Baltzer's reflections.

Included are faces we have seen periodically in academic contexts, some former classmates unmet for years, and those we've encountered for the first time. Our foreshortened process meant that we were not able to contact in time everyone that would have wanted to contribute, and for this we apologize. Each period of Helmut's career as teacher and advisor is nonetheless well represented, and so those who speak here in effect are speaking for many of their classmates as well. Some of the insights we offer are touching, others entertaining, and each valuable in its own way.

The warm and positive tone in this volume is not intended to mask a reality: anyone who has worked with Helmut Koester has had "moments" with him. A person with such exacting standards, eclectic interests, challenging purposes and strong opinions reminds us that "iron sharpening iron" often occurs by friction. Indeed, when considering a title for this volume, "One Helmut and Four Primitive Responses" came to mind. The reader may select four to express her or his own "trajectory" through life seasons and episodes.

Yet all too infrequently do we, as students and scholars, share a moment in which personal, methodological and theological differences leave room for a sincere expression of thanks in community. We hope that the reader will gain fresh appreciation for the quality of Helmut's contributions over the years, and receive pleasure, even a blessing, through this tribute. Specific threads and patterns wind their away across the pages, including the love of music, the warmth of the Koester family table, the growing of cabbages and potatoes, visits to archaeological sites under the hot sun, and of course reminiscences of many still-fresh encounters between student and teacher. Some readers may simply enjoy the stories, while others are struck by the sequence of student generations and metamorphosis in scholarship over the years. Still others will, no doubt, use their critical tools to examine the texts in search of lost sources, odd doublets, or legendary elements. As with the gospels, this is not a snapshot but a portrait, expressing with conviction the importance of a remarkable person.

Helmut Koester has spent a lifetime directing our attention to the specificities of Jesus, the world he entered, and the traditions he inspired. In expressing our gratitude to him, we also offer special thanks to K. C. Hanson and the team at Wipf and Stock Publishers, for catching the vision of this project and bringing it through the demanding process to publication.

—*Philip Sellew and Jim Smith*

Foreword

KRISTER STENDAHL

IT IS some fifty years this August since I picked up Helmut and his family on the Pier in Manhattan. I remember it all so well, also the violin case. And then we drove to Cambridge and Harvard. Together with Amos Wilder—so much our senior and so much wiser—we had the once in a lifetime opportunity to be in on the reviving of the Divinity School as it was given new life—and monies—thanks to the bold support of Nathan Pusey who had become Harvard president in 1953.

With our youthful brashness and a little European arrogance we shaped the program, tone and style of the New Testament graduate work, the fruits of which are the substance of the essays to follow. It seemed natural that all three of us participated in the weekly doctoral seminar—a far from common practice in U.S. education. I believe this turned out to be one of our better ideas. It gave to New Testament studies a distinct tone and strength within the School. It also allowed us faculty to know each other's thinking at the level that really counts, not only by small talk or faculty politics.

Invited to write a foreword in this tribute to *Helmut at 80*—can you believe it?—I thought the time had perhaps come for me to confess a feeling I have harbored for many years—a feeling of envy. It became clearer and clearer to me that there were especially two areas where Helmut excelled—and I did not. (Not to speak about the writing of books.) And the two happen to be key to the work and lives of the grateful contributors to follow.

HELMUT AS SEMINAR LEADER. How does he do it? I have often marveled at how he seemed not to worry about where things were going, allowing a free-for-all, sometimes even a free-fall. And then, somehow, at the end it all comes together so that one goes home with the feeling that something, even some clarity was accomplished. From chaos to cosmos in two hours. That is indeed an art that I never mastered. I find it enviable.

HELMUT AS DISSERTATION DIRECTOR. Here is the other area where Helmut invites my envy: the majestic art of bringing a dissertation safely to birth, staying with it to the end. He seems to know so well that birth is a natural process of creation, and that the midwife is . . . just a midwife. As I look over the list of authors in our volume my envy rekindles, for name after name brings back to me how Helmut mastered the right balance in mixing, directing and enabling, and that is the more impressive considering that he is not known for leaving you in doubt about what he thinks is the right view of things. It is not an accident that by far the majority of Harvard dissertations in our fields 1956–2006 have had Helmut as the major adviser. As midwife of scholars he has raised himself a monument aere perennius.

So, in Helmut's honor I confess my envy. Or must envy always be a sin to be confessed? Can it not also be the pure and simple awareness of a colleague's great gifts? Such envy makes for friendships to last—ad multos annos, dear colleague.

—Krister Stendahl

The Fifties and Sixties

Helmut and Gisela at their wedding, 1953

HELMUT KOESTER has made enormous contributions to the study of the New Testament, its *Umwelt*, and the history of early Christianity. The following words will address these well-known accomplishments only indirectly while reflecting on some more personal impressions.

Helmut belies the image of the cold Germanic scholar. His personable manner, warm smile of greeting, remembrance and knowledge of individuals are refreshing and reassuring.

Most students and colleagues know his exacting demands for scholarship—a source of dismay and even terror to students working under him. He holds the academic world at large to high standards. The result, however, has been careful, comprehensive, and creative productions from himself and from his students that are precise and do indeed advance the boundaries of learning. He continues to take an interest in his students and their careers.

The work of Helmut, his students, and those associated with him has stimulated study by others—even, or perhaps especially, by those who disagreed with him. One commonly learns more from those with whom one disagrees than from those with whom one agrees.

In addition to the influence of Helmut's own writings and guidance of students' research, note should be taken of his promotion of study on the non-literary remains of the Greco-Roman world. One of his important and enduring contributions has been the stimulation of research in the *realia* of the Aegean world, using this material in the interpretation of the New Testament, and making it accessible to wider circles. I am glad to have had a small part in promoting the project that led to *Archaeological Resources for New Testament Studies* (and as a corollary several doctoral dissertations) through providing hospitality, arranging speaking appointments, and introducing potential donors.

Another area in which Helmut has widened the scope of knowledge is in the understanding of extra-canonical literature. I remember in my early days being surprised that top-level New Testament scholars seemed to have such a narrow competence. Their extrabiblical knowledge was limited to a few well- known Jewish texts; their acquaintance with Greek

1

and Latin authors and especially with early Christian writings outside the canon was meager at best. Things are very much different now, and Helmut is one of the persons responsible for broadening the perception of early Christianity. The opposite condition may prevail now, whereby persons with degrees in New Testament know more about other texts than about the New Testament itself, but Helmut is not to be blamed for this circumstance.

The description of Helmut that comes to mind is that he has attempted to be a bridge-builder. Combining the examination of literary with non-literary sources as well as combining the study of canonical with non-canonical writings are only two examples of this. His education in Germany and long teaching career in the U.S. have bridged American and continental scholarship. Lecturing in many countries has multiplied the number of those bridges.

Helmut has had an interest in popularizing the results of scholarship, bridging the academy and the community. His lectures in my hometown of Abilene, Texas, were not only informative but also well received. This is only one example out of many of his going to smaller communities and small schools to speak and lecture. Moreover, he has had an interest and willingness to communicate to churches and so seek to bridge the worlds of the university and the church.

All of these activities are endeavors for which I am very much appreciative.

—*Everett Ferguson*

PROFESSOR DR. Helmut Koester became a major figure in my academic life and scholarly career from the very time of his arrival at the Harvard Divinity School in the Fall of 1958, as I was entering my third year as a Ph.D. student in the Graduate School of Arts and Sciences. Although Krister Stendahl was my official adviser, my committee for both the General Examinations and the dissertation included also Helmut, Amos N. Wilder, and Arthur Darby Nock, each of whom had a profound influence on my development as a scholar. Early on I expressed my gratitude in the preface of my first book (1966): "One is able perhaps to repay so large a debt for patient guidance and individual concern, for academic instruction, scholarly example, and intellectual inspiration only by attempting in some measure to transmit to one's own students that which in full measure was first given by these mentors." Twenty-five years later, in the 1991 *Festschrift* for Helmut, I was somewhat more specific: "To Helmut Koester, a demanding but always supportive mentor and a career-long colleague in *Hermeneia*, I owe far more than can be conveyed in a brief statement that he inspired his students to seek out important issues in early Christianity, to pursue them armed with a thorough grasp of the Greco-Roman world, and to persist in their resolution despite obstacles or opposition." Now fifteen years farther along, our friendship has extended to nearly fifty years, while our *Hermeneia* association has reached its forty-fourth year.

When Helmut arrived at Harvard, I had completed my course work for the Ph.D. degree with Krister Stendahl, Amos Wilder, Visiting Professor John Arthur Thomas Robinson, Frank Moore Cross, Jr., Arthur Darby Nock, Paul Tillich, Richard Reinhold Niebuhr, and Georges Florovsky, as well as Norman K. Gottwald and Paul S. Minear at Andover-Newton Theological School—a quite remarkable way to be drawn into biblical literature and related fields. When Helmut joined the faculty, an opportunity for additional perspectives arose, and I was able to audit his class on "The Gospel Tradition in the Second Century," where Helmut—as all of his students were soon to learn—consistently treated the New Testament writings within the historical continuum of other Christian and contemporary literature and culture, and never as an isolated body of material or a separable entity in late antiquity. Amos Wilder, Krister, and Helmut always attended the weekly New Testament Seminar, required of all doctoral students in residence, where relevant issues were addressed and dissertation progress reports were received. Krister and Helmut were particularly supportive as I worked through my own dissertation. During these several years, as biblical scholarship in Europe was reviving after World War II, a veritable parade of noted scholars lectured at Harvard or nearby, enriching our studies then and our memories later. Among them were Bultmann, Bornkamm, Käsemann, Conzelmann, and Jeremias—representatives of the preceding scholarly generation in Germany, but now, full time, Helmut was on the scene, among the first of the post-war generation of biblical scholars.

Through all these experiences in the expansive Harvard environment, I was captured by the fascination of scholarly investigation and critique. In recent years I often have been asked why Ellie and I retired to Lexington, Massachusetts, and my simple answer has been that we returned to our roots—our *intellectual* roots, for Harvard was the birthplace of our authentic intellectual lives. Helmut, with the others at Harvard, facilitated our rootage during 1955–1961, and upon our return in 1998, he and his biblical colleagues at the Divinity School again extended a warm welcome—completing the circle! The historic town of Lexington is five miles across, and Helmut several times has remarked, in my presence, that I chose to live as far from him as is possible in Lexington! But geographical distance has little to do with collegiality.

If my recollection of one of his own stories is accurate, his mentor, Rudolf Bultmann, after detecting an incorrect Greek accent in Helmut's complex and Greek-laden doctoral dissertation, said to Helmut, "You don't know Greek very well, do you?" History repeated itself, more or less, in my own experience with Helmut. During the Spring of 1958, as expected, I had scheduled my Ph.D. examination in Hellenistic Greek with Krister Stendahl. The day before the exam I encountered Krister in the corridor of Andover Hall, and he said, "By the way, for your Greek examination tomorrow, you will please report to Professor Koester." Puzzled, I presume that I said, "Yes, sir," though my first rush of thought and emotion was apprehension—or to be blunt, fear!—for this young professor just thrust upon us was, after all, a student of the greatest New Testament scholar of the time, and I was on the eve of being examined by him, unexpectedly, in Greek. But what was to fear? I had studied Greek in some formal fashion for the preceding eleven years, so I appeared for the oral test with a mixture of confidence in my knowledge but dread of the unknown. Helmut greeted me by offering a copy of *The Jewish War* by Josephus and asked me to read the first sentence. My eyes scanned that sentence, and its Greek covered the whole page! [Look it up! In the Loeb edition the sentence actually runs two pages, with a footnote commenting on its length.] My memory, perhaps distorted, is that I translated reasonably well and then was asked to translate several other portions of Hellenistic Greek over the next hour with, I thought, rather decent success, given the circumstances and the fair number of passages I had not seen before. Helmut then looked up and, in a rather convoluted fashion, indicated that I had passed the exam, for he said, "Now you have a beginning for the study of Greek." I expressed my thanks and left, wondering what multiples of eleven years might imply a measure of mastery in the Greek language. Helmut, however, was quite correct: there was much more for me to learn—and there still is.

In the mid-1960s, when I was on the faculty of the University of Southern California, Helmut, Gisela, and their family—then two daughters—traveled across the entire country in their trusty Mercedes-Benz, camping along the way and then spending a few days in our home and on the extensive Redondo Beach, a few blocks down the hill. Here our families began a long friendship.

Then in 1964, at the special 100th Meeting of SBL in New York City, Helmut arranged for me to meet Kurt Aland, one of the major speakers, and the three of us spent two hours or more having a drink (or two!) while discussing manuscripts, textual criticism, and a range of other topics. To spend this much time with the Münster scholar who quickly became the leading New Testament textual critic of the twentieth century was an unparalleled boon for a young scholar just entering the field—and a benefit that perhaps Helmut alone could have provided.

The project that would become *Hermeneia* began already in 1962, and I was appointed—undoubtedly at Helmut's suggestion—as Executive Secretary of the New Testament Editorial Board, with full Board membership in 1966 when Fortress Press adopted the fledgling commentary series. From that point on, Helmut served as chair of the New Testament Board, consisting originally also of Robert W. Funk, James M. Robinson, and me, but joined soon after by George W. MacRae, S.J., and considerably later by Harold W. Attridge, Adela Yarbro Collins, and Hans-Josef Klauck. There should be "many a tale to tell" of this long-standing *Hermeneia* project, but in actuality there are few to relate, for the routine business of deciding on the *Hermeneia* name, constructing a style sheet, and approving a new and creative format were carried out without incident. More difficult was selecting European volumes for translation to launch the series and assigning authors for fresh commentaries. As some will know, we did cause an international academic crisis of sorts when we chose not to translate Käsemann's *Romans*, but we were merely following our requirement—reinforced by Helmut's strong emphasis—that *Hermeneia* commentaries be fully informed by *religionsgeschichtliche* material relevant to the New Testament and related literature. Robert Funk left the Board in 1987, transferring his scholarly vision and energy to his Westar Institute, and George MacRae, too, left the Board (in 1985), but only by his untimely death at the very height of his career and influence.

The *Hermeneia* Board also felt more directly than others the ups and downs and ups of Fortress Press over the years, but Helmut's status as a Lutheran minister and his persuasive powers provided a special entrée to the Lutheran board responsible for the Press, and he was always available to fly to Philadelphia or Minneapolis to make certain that *Hermeneia* remained the flagship of Fortress's biblical publication program. Other stories, however, are few because never have I collaborated with a more focused group of scholars working congenially and harmoniously with singular dedication to achieve an ambitious goal—a sophisticated critical and historical biblical commentary that now approaches forty published volumes, with a large number yet to follow. Helmut's central role in this achievement will forever be part of his noteworthy legacy.

Another group experience that Helmut and I shared was the "New Testament Colloquium," a self-perpetuated body of scholars patterned after the German post-Bultmannian *Neutestamentlicher Arbeitskreis* comprised (in 1965) of Hans Conzelmann, Dieter Georgi, Erich Grässer, Ferdinand Hahn, Günter Klein, Walter Schmithals, Georg Strecker, Ulrich Wilkens, and Wolfgang Schrage. The American group, founded in 1960 for the purpose of pursuing issues raised by Bultmann, included Kendrick Grobel, Hans Jonas, and Amos Wilder as "senior members" and Robert Funk, Helmut, James Robinson, and several others as younger members. Dieter Georgi transferred to the American group when he came to the USA in 1964/1965, the same year I was invited to join. The membership grew to nineteen by 1975, including Hans Dieter Betz, Raymond Brown, Joseph Fitzmyer, Victor Furnish, Edward Hobbs, Robert Kraft, George MacRae, Norman Perrin, John Strugnell, and others. About two years later, however, the Colloquium ceased to exist, undoubtedly due, at least in part, to the revolutionary changes in the nature of SBL during the several preceding years when Robert Funk was executive secretary of the Society (1968–1974), followed by George MacRae (1975–1976)—changes in which numerous members of the Colloquium had been activists. In short, what the Colloquium fostered had been replaced by the new Society structures, namely, encouraging discussion and scholarship in small groups but now on a wide range of subjects, thus rendering the Colloquium superfluous. Also, some of us were becoming sensitive to the appearance of elitism inherent in this self-perpetuating group.

There were scholars, of course, who were unwilling to embrace and reluctant to discuss Bultmann's views and, indeed, were threatened by them. For example, I have it on good authority that, as a finalist for a seminary opening, which would have been my first academic position, I was not appointed because, as a student of Helmut, I was guilty by association of being a dreaded "Bultmannian."

A memorable discussion in the Colloquium involved presentations and debate in 1973 by Norman Perrin and Helmut over their forthcoming "Introductions" to the New Testament. This discussion reinforced for me the aptness of Helmut's treatment of the writings that were to become the New Testament within their broad historical, literary, and *religionsgeschichtliche* contexts in the Greco-Roman world, and the wisdom of his departure from the traditional structure and genre of existing "Introductions." It seems so natural and normal now—how else would one/could one treat or understand the collection we call the New Testament? My own teaching, graduate and later undergraduate, flowed readily from within that paradigm, and my specialized studies in textual criticism have moved decisively to a contextual approach as I have tried to see the broad geographical, historical, and socio-cultural environments of our New Testament manuscripts and their variants. We are all indebted to Helmut for his masterful exemplification of this approach. Without it, would we have the images, insights, and interpretations to be found in his *Ancient Christian Gospels* or his magnificent *Cities of Paul*?

In 1971 the members of the Colloquium, who were well aware of Norman Perrin's chronic illness, presented to him a small *Festschrift* celebrating his fiftieth birthday. Six of us, including Helmut, reviewed and discussed various of Perrin's writings, and this volume, *Christology and a Modern Pilgrimage: A Discussion with Norman Perrin*, was in actuality the first publication of what almost immediately thereafter was to become Scholars' Press.

This brief narrative, however, not only is incapable of conveying the early and continuing support offered by Helmut to me and to many others, but also falls drastically short in its attempt to relate the career-long scholarly influences and interactions that he has provided. Nor has it conveyed in any adequate fashion the friendship we have shared. Altogether, our mutual journey became an unusually rich mentor-student and later a collegial relationship of a half-century duration, of which I am very much the beneficiary.

—*Eldon Epp*

I HAD ALREADY reached the Harvard Graduate School of Arts and Sciences, program in the History and Philosophy of Religion, when Helmut Koester arrived in the fall of 1958. Helmut who? His reported status as the last of Rudolf Bultmann's graduate students gave him a foot in the door of instant fame among us sometimes cynical young grad students (we did know who Bultmann was!), although getting used to his rapidly improving American speech patterns was sometimes amusing as well as challenging. One of his first graduate assistants, Bill Lane, sometimes helped locate the right words and expressions for him.

My own interests lay in early Christian uses of Jewish sources and traditions, so the fact that Helmut had worked not only with early gospel traditions in the Apostolic Fathers, but also with Justin's use of Jewish Greek biblical materials was attractive. His course in second-century gospel traditions helped set a direction for me that led to my own dissertation on the Epistle of Barnabas, as well as a deepened attraction for things text-critical and tradition-critical.

Social occasions at the Divinity School—especially the annual Yuletide party (we called it "Christmas" back then)—provided us with opportunities to get to know Helmut and his colleagues better. If we had slight trouble with Helmut's American English, it was even worse with Arthur Darby Nock's British English! Once Helmut was heard to comment to the effect that his understanding of Nock's speech was enhanced proportionately with the amount of alcohol each imbibed. After a few drinks, he could at least understand some of what Nock was saying. Those of us who didn't drink alcohol were at a definite disadvantage, it would seem.

We also got to know Helmut for his brief mentions of how he found himself in the German navy at the close of World War II, as a seventeen -year old draftee (if I'm remembering correctly). My own German ancestry, and juvenile fascination with war experiences, made this part of Helmut's youth all the more memorable, to be combined later with similar reflections from Gerhard Kroedel (then at the Lutheran Seminary in Philadelphia) on his experiences in the German air force at the war's end. Indeed, Helmut's conditioning as a youth in Hitler's Germany along with his efforts to master spoken English contributed to the memorable, if embarrassing moment, when he forcefully told the class to "remember, Chesus vas a gud Cherman … [Bill Lane signals wildly from the back of the room] uh, Chew." It was, of course, a moment to forget; but for me it underlined the deeply personal transitions that were taking place in Helmut's move to this radically different time and space.

Perhaps the most amusing Helmut story in those early years was his report about his motor trip to Syracuse to hear his *Doktorvater*, Rudolf Bultmann, during the latter's 1958–1959 visit. While Helmut was returning along the New York Thruway, doubtless driving at autobahn speeds, to his amazement a large bird suddenly crashed through his windshield. Helmut was shaken but unhurt, and glanced back to discover the remains of "a peasant" in the back seat. At that we could all laugh—Helmut included—and we did, and still do in retrospect. It was doubtless a rather ordinary New York country pheasant—with a bad flight pattern to boot!

Sometimes, when Helmut was out of earshot (I hope), some students (not me!) referred to him jokingly by alluding to his physical stature with a linguistic twist—"der Kleinste." Coincidentally, perhaps, this could also be seen as a religious compliment of sorts (see Matt 11:11). In any event, I know of no-one who would have directed such an epithet at Helmut's pedagogical or intellectual or supportive size. My best memories are of the encouragement and assistance and *Gemütlichkeit* that we were favored to receive from Helmut, on his way to becoming a valued and abiding fixture in John Harvard's hallowed house.

> When you came to these shores
>> books in one hand, violin in the other,
>>> what did you expect, or plan?
> Might it become a stepping stone
>> to a triumphal return back home?

> Fortunately, it didn't play out that way.

Robert A. Kraft

Germany's loss proved to be our gain
    and we laud you for staying the course;
It must not have been easy, at times,
    but you find sustenance in challenges
        and this "other bread" has fed us all.

—RAK

WHEN I arrived at Harvard University Graduate School of Arts and Sciences in the fall of 1957 to pursue a Ph.D. in the History and Philosophy of Religion, I was, at twenty-one years of age, the youngest person in the program and the only one with just an undergraduate B.A. degree. Most of the students in the Ph.D. and Th.D. programs were a decade or two older than I, and everyone had some kind of advanced degree.

I often felt like a fish out of water, especially in my first year in the graduate program. Although I had had five years of French, four years of Latin, and a year each of Biblical Hebrew and Classical Greek before I arrived at Harvard, I had studied no German, except for two months of private lessons with a very talented polyglot language teacher in my native Brooklyn, New York, during the summer of 1957 following my graduation from Princeton and before my arrival at Harvard.

The fall of 1958 brought an important addition to the faculty of the Harvard Divinity School, an addition that changed my professional focus and ultimately my career. A thirty-year young Helmut Koester arrived on campus, and my faculty advisor Krister Stendahl recommended that I enroll in the new professor's two-semester course in gospel tradition in the second century.

Helmut spoke little English when he arrived at Harvard in the fall of 1958, and I spoke even less German. His initial lectures, presumably translated into English by a native speaker, were difficult for me to follow. His accent was heavy, and his very formal lectures that fall were delivered with little sense that Professor Koester fully understood what he was reading. I tried to follow the subject matter of the course more closely by reading Helmut's *Synoptische Überlieferung bei den Apostolischen Vätern*, happily available at the Divinity School bookstore. I'm not sure, however, which was the greater challenge, understanding Helmut's English that first semester or trying to read his magnum opus in German.

Helmut was very patient with me, and I loved the subject matter of the year-long course. By the spring semester of 1959, Professor Koester's English had improved markedly. Helmut took me under his wing and recommended that I spend the summer semester of 1959 at Heidelberg University in Germany taking courses with the *Theologische Fakultät*. He even helped me write the requisite essay in German in order to complete my application for the program at Heidelberg.

When I arrived in Germany in June of 1959 at the tender age of twenty-three, Helmut helped me find suitable housing for the summer in Heidelberg at a tiny garden house, which I subsequently learned had previously been a chicken house, in the hills on the opposite side of the Neckar River. The house faced the legendary Heidelberg University and the imposing Heidelberg Castle. The view was exhilarating; the summer was exciting; and the climb up the steep hill to my garden house twice a day was enormously challenging. During the course of that summer, I attended a lecture course by Gerhard von Rad, and an advanced seminar on the Epistle of James with Günther Bornkamm. I'm not sure how much of the material I understood, but my spoken German improved considerably over the course of that summer, and I had the honor of auditing courses from two of the most distinguished biblical scholars of the twentieth century. On a weekend early in that summer, Helmut drove me to Hamburg for a weekend to visit the family of a friend I had met during the previous fall in Cambridge, Massachusetts. A very personal touch by a very generous man!

When I arrived back at Harvard in the fall of 1959, I was far more confident of myself, and far better prepared to take my German exam, a prerequisite for the Ph.D. and for the numerous books in German that I would subsequently have to read as I prepared my doctoral dissertation on *The Sayings of Jesus in the Writings of Justin Martyr*, completed in 1962 under Helmut's supervision. That work was subsequently published by E. J. Brill in 1967 and earned me my initial reputation as a young New Testament scholar. To the extent that this book has been well received over the last four decades, a great deal of the credit goes to Helmut Koester, who worked on it laboriously with me through several drafts. I was among Helmut's first doctoral students at Harvard, possibly the first to actually receive the Harvard Ph.D.

My next professional work with Helmut was the translation from German into English of his "Geschichte und Kultus im Johannesevangelium und bei Ignatius von Antiochien" as "History and Cult in the Gospel of John and in Ignatius of Antioch," in *The Bultmann School of Biblical Interpretation: New Directions.*

Professor William R. Farmer of Southern Methodist University read my book on Justin Martyr with interest and phoned me at home one day to engage me in trying to identify the criteria that Justin Martyr had used in creating his harmonization of the texts of the gospels of Matthew and Luke, apparently hoping that my work on the subject would convince scholars of the priority of the Gospel of Matthew. Farmer hoped that Justin's method of harmonizing the gospels of Matthew and Luke into a single document would support his own position on the conflation of the gospels of Matthew and Luke by the author of the Gospel of Mark. My work with Bill Farmer led ultimately to my editing the collection of essays in *The Two-Source Hypothesis: A Critical Appraisal*, but, to Farmer's disappointment, it did not lead me to embrace Farmer's commitment to the Griesbach Hypothesis. Like Helmut, I remain convinced of the priority of the Gospel of Mark.

Farmer also asked me to oversee the translation into English of Édouard Massaux's *The Influence of the Gospel of Saint Matthew on Christian Literature before Saint Irenaeus* (3 volumes). Farmer and I also hoped that we could translate into English Helmut Koester's influential *Synoptische Überlieferung* as the principal alternative to Massaux's position; however, Helmut was convinced that he had by that time already provided in English everything that was relevant on the subject in his monumental *Introduction to the New Testament*, volume one: *History, Culture, and Religion in the Hellenistic Age*; volume two: *History and Literature of Early Christianity.*

More recently I was honored to share a platform with Helmut Koester at the Oxford Conference on the New Testament and the Apostolic Fathers, held at Lincoln College, Oxford in April of 2004. Helmut delivered the major address at the conference: "Gospels and Gospel Traditions in the Second Century." I delivered a more modest paper on "The Gospel of Luke in the Apostolic Fathers," contrasting primarily the positions of Helmut Koester and Édouard Massaux on the subject. Our essays were printed sequentially in the volume *Trajectories through the New Testament and the Apostolic Fathers*.

Perhaps even more important about that conference, at least for me, was spending quality time once again with Professor Koester. We took several meals together at the conference dining hall and had a chance to speak in ways in which we had not spoken since I was a graduate student at Harvard in the late fifties and early sixties, when Helmut and I were both still very young.

Yet, what I never told Helmut, although it should be evident to anyone who knows me and my work, is the enormous debt of gratitude that I owe to Helmut Koester for my professional career. Helmut Koester was the quintessential teacher/scholar for that ingenuous man in his young twenties in Cambridge, Massachusetts during the years 1958–1962, and I am forever indebted to him for serving as a mentor to me for those four years, and for the four and a half decades since our days together at Harvard. Helmut Koester's lifetime contribution to New Testament studies is enormous. His contribution to my life and my career is immeasurable. Thank you, Helmut.

—*Arthur Bellinzoni*

I TRANSFERRED INTO the S.T.B. program at Harvard Divinity School in the fall of 1959 in order to study with Krister Stendahl. To my dismay, he turned out to be on leave for that academic year. To my delight, on the other hand, I found myself studying under Helmut Koester, who would be my principal mentor until 1967, when I completed my Ph.D. dissertation. Those of us who were students at HDS during this period may have somewhat different views of our experience, but I think we all would agree that the faculty, newly formed under Dean Miller and President Pusey, was superb and the intellectual climate as stimulating as it was demanding. A large part of the stimulation came from the diversity of the faculty and the different kinds of things they were working on. But equally important was the fact that the field of New Testament studies was itself in a state of ferment as a result of the ongoing discoveries of the Dead Sea Scrolls and the Nag Hammadi library, discoveries that put to question presumably settled issues in the study of early Christianity. I recall the title of an article that appeared in the early sixties: "New Texts, New Questions, New Methods." In the face of all this newness, including new faculty, New Testament studies at Harvard became a problem solving enterprise, forcing us all to focus more on evidence and arguments than on previous solutions to problems that now appeared in a new light. I for one loved every minute of it.

Helmut's genius in all of this is perhaps best represented in an assessment he was delighted to offer when asked to compare German graduate students to their American counterparts. Helmut responded by saying that they both had in common a passionate concern for the truth, the difference being that American students believed that "the truth was to be found where the professor was not." Helmut's genius was that, having recognized the difference, he learned to cultivate it in his teaching by forcing us to show him the truths we thought we had found, rather than telling us what the truth was. Thus did the former German graduate student become an American Professor, and my *Doktorvater*.

In this light, I find it somewhat ironic that Helmut's great indebtedness to his teacher, Rudolf Bultmann, and to the German academic tradition generally, led me to spend years exploring that tradition in depth, studying the work of Bultmann, Johannes Weiss, William Wrede, Hermann Gunkel, and Martin Dibelius, in order to see how they defined problems and resolved them. As I said in comments made at the presentation of a *Festschrift* honoring Helmut's sixty-fifth birthday, he introduced me to my extended academic family, in which Bultmann became my grandfather and Weiss my great-grandfather, to which genealogy I would like to add Wrede as the closest of cousins. So Helmut both opened my mind up to the new and introduced me to a past that enabled me to grasp and come to grips with the new. So effective was he in opening up the academic past that in my dissertation oral exams Krister Stendahl remarked that he was surprised to find that the scholars I held in highest regard had all been dead for fifty years. (Or was it: "You don't have anything good to say about scholars who haven't been dead for years"?) Fortunately for me none of the Harvard faculty had written on Irenaeus and the Apocryphon of John!

While my subsequent research tended more and more to new methods required to handle the new questions raised by the new evidence, Helmut's ongoing influence on my work was perhaps strongest in my teaching. In the things I have published I have entertained insights made possible by methods and theories from other disciplines, such as literary criticism, social anthropology, and the sociology of language and knowledge. All of this of course made its way into my teaching. But whether teaching the Old Testament or the New, my focus was in large part on the history of traditions (and texts) made visible by the form criticism to which Helmut had so persuasively introduced me. Similarly, his insistence on ignoring canonical restrictions when analyzing traditions and texts, and on understanding their history of religious contexts, governed my teaching throughout an almost thirty-five-year career. It is at least in part a sign of my respect for Helmut that I rarely published any of this, although my students and some editors of *JBL*, for whom I reviewed over forty papers, could attest to my indebtedness to Helmut for all that he taught me—and for which I am eternally grateful.

So, a very happy 80th birthday, Helmut. I don't know which I am more proud of: having had you as my *Doktorvater*, or having had you as my successor at Williams College, if only for a year. Cheers.

—*Norman Petersen*

I REMEMBER HELMUT Koester both as a scholar and teacher and as a human being and friend. Here a just a few frames snipped from a longer and richer reel.

During my first semester as a graduate student at Harvard we were treated to Helmut's first take on "The History of Early Christianity." It was to be the first of a two-semester course that would span the first two centuries of the church's history. What was new for me was the treatment of the New Testament, not as a book or collection of books or a canon, but as a series of witnesses to the history of a religious community. This would affect me in several important ways during the three decades of my own teaching career at Iowa and thereafter. Helmut's two-semester sequence was the model for a similar sequence that I and my colleague Jim McCue taught together more than a half-dozen times; and that course, in turn, was enriched when Helmut published his two-volume history, which became the text for our course. It also governed the approach in my annual undergraduate "Introduction to the New Testament." Furthermore, along with Barney Anderson's *Understanding the Old Testament*, it provided a structure for my *Jewish Literature Between the Bible and the Mishnah*. Post-Helmut, my approach to the texts was always historical, even if, thanks to my good friend Norman Petersen, it was also literary in character.

When it can time for the dissertation, I was fortunate to have an active committee of four persons (Krister Stendahl as my advisor, Helmut, Frank Cross, and John Strugnell). All of them read each chapter as I wrote it, and that made it easier when I put them together. Helmut—though he was not my adviser—always read my material carefully and provided written, to-the-point comments, some of which I still have on their yellow lined pages. I recall a couple of incidents that particularly affected the dissertation and its aftermath. As I sat in his library office and showed him one of my charts, he exclaimed, "You have discovered the *Gattung* of the passion narrative!" (It took fifteen years with Helmut's prodding before that observation became incarnate in an *HTR* article.) More important for the dissertation, it was Helmut who pointed me to

19

Klaus Baltzer's work on the Deutero-Isaianic Servant *qua* prophet. This significantly shaped part of my second chapter by providing a rationale for the Wisdom of Solomon/Servant connection that had previously not been noted in the literature.

Perhaps most significant for my career was an early SBL meeting in New York City. The Society was inventing and proliferating interest groups and seminars. It was my moment of truth. I asked Helmut: Do I continue to re-rake the soil of the New Testament, or do I try to break new ground in the non-canonical texts. Being a wise and non-provincial mentor, he pointed me in the direction that determined my three-and-a-half decades of scholarship—knowing, I suspect, it would have some implications for the interpretation of early Christianity.

As to the other side of Helmut . . . In the summer of 1962 or 1963, Helmut was taking his family and his Volkswagen camper to Europe. It was the year of the great rust, when most Massachusetts license plates had turned reddish brown. Helmut, of course, didn't want to drive the *Autobahnen* with illegible plates. Somehow he discovered I could work a wire brush and a paintbrush, and so he invited me to scrape and re-letter his plates (something no professor would think of doing these days).

Very different was when Helmut—a photographer of no mean skills—invited himself, as a gift to Marilyn and me, to take the photographs of our wedding. There was a bit of a New Testament tug-of-war that today, with Helmut upstairs restaging the ceremony, and Krister—in something of a hurry to get to his next engagement—waiting downstairs to invoke the Deity before the reception. A couple of weeks later Helmut and I spent an evening in his darkroom printing out the pictures.

And so, Helmut, I remember and salute you warmly and with many good wishes for the years to come.

—*George Nickelsburg*

THERE IS only one Helmut Koester . . .

My first semester at Harvard was Fall, 1962, and began against the backdrop of great national angst arising from the Cuban missile crisis, with JFK and Nikita Kruschev on opposing sides of the chess-board. While I was not officially enrolled in Helmut's classes that semester, I was an eager auditor, and recall the passion with which he took his stand on that critical issue.

It was during the second semester, when Helmut directed the New Testament Seminar, that I had the first opportunity to experience his reaction to my work. I had come to Harvard with a reasonably good education in theology and philology, but it soon became clear that I had much to learn. The focus of the seminar that semester was Paul's Thessalonian correspondence, and my paper was devoted to a study of 2 Thessalonians 2:1–12. It was a rather mediocre paper, and one of its problems was my uncritical acceptance of that epistle's Pauline authorship. Helmut was kinder than he could have been in appraising my work at that time. Of course, I eventually revised my approach to the Thessalonian letters, and am glad to say that my article, "1 Thessalonians 2:13–16: A Deutero-Pauline Interpolation," published in *HTR* in 1971, met with Helmut's approval.

In one respect I came too early to Harvard. I was his first student to elect archaeology as the sixth area for my General Examinations, taken in Spring, 1964. At that time, Helmut had no particular interest in archaeology, and in preparation for the exam I concentrated on Palestinian archaeology in the Roman period, working with Ernest Wright and Nahman Avigad. Helmut's interest in archaeology began in the 1970s, and I came to envy those Harvard students who accompanied Helmut on his archaeological surveys in Greece and Asia Minor.

I must say that one of the best memories I have of Helmut during my student days was the care with which he read and annotated each draft of a chapter of my dissertation as it was submitted to him. For me, he was not only a model scholar, and a brilliant teacher but also a wonderful *Doktorvater*. And I'm sure the many other students who were his *Kinder* during his 40 years of teaching at Harvard feel the same way.

Of course, I have other fond memories of Helmut during those student years. One of these is the hospitality extended by him and Gisela to Karen and me in their home on several occasions. Another is the wonderful experience of sharing with others in their home on Good Friday as we listened to Bach's *St. Matthew Passion*, joining the chorus in singing the choral sections of that wonderful cantata. That is a practice that I later adopted myself in Durham, North Carolina, and then in Santa Barbara.

When I left Harvard and began full-time teaching, first at Duke and then at UC Santa Barbara, it was Helmut Koester who was for me the model scholar-teacher whom I tried to emulate in my own work in teaching and scholarly research. And when, finally, his magisterial two-volume *Einführung* was published in English in 1982, I naturally adopted it as required reading for students in my courses on Origins of Christianity, Second-Century Christianity, and Hellenistic Religions. My students contributed mightily to Helmut's royalty income!

Back in the "old" days, there was a kind of "rite of passage" for a new doctor. Helmut Koester and Krister Stendahl were no longer to be addressed as "Professor" or "Doctor," but now as "Helmut" and "Krister." This was a sign that former teachers had now become colleagues. So, yes, Helmut became my colleague, but he is still my teacher, and dear friend.

Over the years it was always a joy for me and my roommates at the annual SBL meeting, George Nickelsburg and Norman Petersen, to share time with Helmut and Gisela, sometimes in our hotel room over Scotch or Bourbon, but often in the famous "Fortress Suite," where scholars of all ages and numerous countries made and renewed acquaintances. (Unfortunately, the "Fortress Suite" no longer exists, a real loss to many of us "old-timers.") Helmut and Gisela were probably there one evening at the annual Meeting in Atlanta in 1986. In any case, George Nickelsburg, Norman Petersen, Tom Kraabel, and I met that evening with Fortress Press Director Hal Rast in his bedroom in the suite to discuss a new publishing project, a *Festschrift* for Helmut five years hence when he would turn 65. The plan was to have the *Festschrift* ready for presentation at the

Annual Meeting of SBL in 1991, and I was "elected" by my colleagues to serve as Editor, a real privilege for me. Of course, the others collaborated with me in the project.

The *Festschrift* was presented to Helmut at the Harvard Divinity School Reception at the Annual Meeting in Kansas City, November 1991. Appropriately enough, Helmut was SBL President that year. The *Festschrift* contains an epilogue by Helmut himself entitled "Current Issues in New Testament Scholarship." The text of the epilogue is an address given by Helmut to a group of Lutheran professors at the 1990 Annual Meeting of the SBL in New Orleans, and was surreptitiously supplied to me by Michael West, then Senior Editor at Fortress Press (and a former student of mine at UCSB). Thus, unbeknownst to him until its appearance, Helmut got the last word in his own *Festschrift*.

Helmut retired from full-time teaching at Harvard after forty years of service on the faculty in 1998. His colleagues organized a special program for Helmut in May, where he would present a farewell lecture. The lecture was entitled "The Community of the New Age: Paul's Letters as a New Political Theology for Christian Community." I was honored to be invited to that program with a lecture on "The Significance of Helmut Koester's Work for Scholarship in Christian Origins." In that lecture I commented on the wide scope of Helmut's scholarship, on his work on early Christian gospels and gospel traditions, with special attention to his work on canonical Mark and the *Secret Gospel of Mark* and on "Q" and *Thomas*, on his work on early Christian diversity, and his contributions in the field of early Christian and Aegean archaeology. I also ventured some comments on his attitude toward new scholarly methods, and the central place of the historical-critical approach in the study of early Christianity. I offered the text of the lecture for publication in the *Harvard Divinity Bulletin*, but it was rejected by the Editor. So I published a version of it in the Lutheran theological journal, *dialog* ("Helmut Koester: Exemplary Scholar and Teacher," Winter 1999).

As part of my preparation for my lecture at Harvard, I checked the "author" section in the electronic catalog "Melvyl," which contains publications in all of the University of California libraries plus the Graduate Theological Union in Berkeley. Of twenty-three records listed for "Koester,

Helmut," entry no. 10 was a dissertation entitled, "Die deutsche Herren-bekleidungsindustrie: Möglichkeiten und Grenzen der Verbandsbildung in einer saison-und modebedingten Fertigwarenindustrie," Berlin, 1932 (roughly translated: "The German men's-clothing industry: possibilities and limitations for union organizing in a seasonal and fashion-dependent ready-to-wear industry"), published when our Helmut was six years old. Could there really be another Helmut Koester?

Well, for us, his students, colleagues, and friends, there is only one Helmut Koester.

Dear Helmut, we congratulate you on your 80th birthday and wish you continued good health and productivity in the years to come.

—*Birger Pearson*

A RRIVING AT Harvard excited and uncertain—anomalous, as a woman in the doctoral program—I realized while listening to Helmut Koester's lecture in Sperry Hall that I was in the right place—challenged, intrigued, and inspired. That Helmut loves teaching was obvious—and many of us were surprised to discover how amazingly generous he is with his time, not only in seminars, and outside of them, but often inviting students to dinner with the family. As we all know, his classic articles and books have broken new ground in the field; and those of us fortunate enough to be among his students know how he often raised questions that catalyzed—and impelled—discovery. We enjoy his intellectual curiosity and pleasure in discovery that invited us along for the ride—exploring not only New Testament sources, but the uncharted terrain of the Nag Hammadi codices.

Recently, seeing Helmut and Gisela at Harvard and at professional meetings, I have come to appreciate him especially for that characteristic generosity—especially after seeing that not everyone who has achieved great scholarly distinction, takes delight, as he does, in current debates, and enjoys celebrating his students' successes. That so many of his students all over the country—and the world—have made major contributions to scholarship in early Christianity owes much to Helmut's energy, his capacity for intellectual curiosity, and his great generosity of spirit. For all of this, we deeply thank—and celebrate—him!

—Elaine Pagels

The Sixties and Seventies

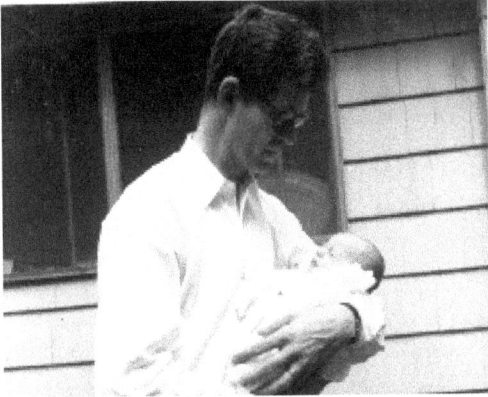

Krister Stendahl with his godson
Ulrich Koester, 1962

Krister Stendahl, Gisela, and the
Koester children

WHEN I received the news that a collection of tributes was being prepared in honor of Professor Helmut Koester on the occasion of his 80th birthday this December, I was grateful to receive an invitation to offer my own personal tribute. I am thankful to Professor Koester's former students for taking on such a good initiative, as my memories of Helmut Koester are very pleasant ones which speak to my relationship with him on both scholarly and personal levels. My encounter with Professor Koester in a scholarly capacity goes back to 1965, when I began my Ph.D. studies at Harvard. Throughout my studies, he served as my doctoral advisor. Indeed, I believe that it may safely be asserted that Professor Koester "produced" more holders of doctoral degrees under his advisement than any other professor in his field during his time at Harvard. In many ways, he was much more than my advisor; he was a dear friend whose own commitment to academic excellence was truly inspirational.

Helmut Koester's commitment to rigor and academic excellence was coupled with an acute and remarkable sensitivity to social concerns and to humanitarian efforts for the afflicted of this world. I remember him as always being aware of the frailty of human existence and the many personal struggles which human beings are confronted with on a regular basis. This remarkable sensitivity was a manifestation not only of his pursuit of truth, but also of his commitment to Christian faith and life that he encouraged others to embrace by example.

In 1972, after my returning to Athens, I remember accompanying Professor Koester with a number of his HDS students to Greece, when he began his truly innovative New Testament archaeological project visiting the cities of St. Paul. This has been a long-standing project which became quite popular with students over the past three decades. I was well aware of his scholarly acumen and interest regarding this arena of research and study, but it was during the first journey with him to places of Greece when I witnessed his sincere passion for his work, his healthy spirit of engaging in demanding tasks, and his rightly held belief that the New Testament world of the past was, for all intents and purposes of scholarship, very much a world alive and well. His academic pursuits in Greece affected a wide array of divinity students at Harvard, and I know that several significant doctoral dissertations were produced as a result of the summer programs which he had initiated visiting the cities of St. Paul, the program having had eventually expanded into some of the cities of modern day Turkey related to St. Paul's journeys. My direct connection with Professor Koester on a professional level took on another dimension when I served as a visiting professor at Harvard, first in 1984–1985, and later in 1988–1989. During these periods, Helmut was always available in his usual invigorating manner, and our collaborative work on various scholarly pursuits continued to develop. More importantly, our friendship with one another continued to deepen.

Indeed, some of the fondest memories I have of Helmut are of those times spent with his endearing family. He used to invite us frequently as doctoral students to his home in Lexington, Massachusetts, where his wonderful wife Gisela would graciously offer a joyful family dinner followed by long discussions on New Testament issues, and many times ending with musical performances by the quintet of the entire Koester family. I cannot forget one summer in Greece when my late father and mother, who were particularly fond of the Koester family, hosted a dinner at our home in the suburb of Neo Psychiko, northeast of Athens, for Helmut and his family. After dinner, the Koester family—having brought with them their musical instruments: viola, violins, and flute—began playing for us some exquisite pieces of classical music. So there, all of a sudden, we found ourselves being treated to an impromptu concerto performance of an amazing quality. The next morning my neighbors were wondering which company had performed such a totally unexpected private performance of music, and if this ensemble was available for hire, as the whole of my neighborhood had also heard the sounds of this dreamlike and impromptu nocturne.

Helmut Koester's associations with my own country of origin also struck a special chord in my heart. They had a personal effect upon him and his children in ways with which I could identify. In fact, his first daughter stayed in Greece for a number of years, and she developed the ability to speak the Greek language to native proficiency. I was rather moved to see that I could relate so personally to others like Helmut and his extraordinary wife Gisela, and their beloved four children, Elli, Ulrich, Almut, and Heiko, who shared my close affiliations with two countries in which I have lived and which I will always love: Greece and the United States. So here too, there was an immediate connection of a personal nature that I found in my relationship with Professor Koester and his family.

I could certainly go on and on regarding other memories of mine concerning Professor Koester, on both scholarly and personal levels. It is necessary however, if only for the sake of length, that I close this reflection in humble tribute to Helmut Koester, my great friend and most distinguished professor. I close it with a final expression of thanksgiving to God for blessing him abundantly for eighty years, and with a wholehearted prayer that the Lord grant him many, many more happy and creative years. I am also grateful to God for the opportunity to know this great man as a superb scholar and as a precious friend, and I am thankful to his students who were so considerate to arrange for the production of this collection of tributes. It has given all of us the important opportunity to spend some quality moments of reflection about a remarkable man who has enriched and continues to enrich the lives of so many.

—Demetrios Trakatellis †

IMAGINE A conservative young man in the mid-1960s coming to Harvard for doctoral work (many of my acquaintances thought this would be destructive of my faith) and then studying with my mentor Helmut Koester, a student of Bultmann! I did come with some genuine fear and trembling, but it was not really such a difficult transition. I had received a very fine education at Wheaton College (where, by the way, Bob Kraft was my introduction to philosophy teacher) and at Gordon Divinity School, where my three New Testament professors were all doctoral graduates of Harvard. My transition to Harvard was also helped by the genuine welcome I received from Helmut.

I learned so much from Helmut in terms of the study of the broad field of New Testament studies. All of my teaching in my career has been deeply shaped by my commitment to attempt to understand texts in their social, cultural and religious contexts, a passion shaped to a very large degree by Helmut.

Helmut introduced me in new and deeper ways to second-century Christian literature, which remains a central focus of my teaching and research (including "gnosticism"). In more recent years I have taught doctoral seminars on second-century Christian literature, the Apostolic Fathers, the Apocryphal New Testament, and am planning one on non-canonical gospels. In all of these ventures I am deeply indebted to Helmut, whose "presence" is real when I teach such seminars.

Helmut also developed my interests in Greco-Roman religions and pushed me to take a course in the Classics Department with Albrecht Dihle and a course in Rabbinic Hebrew with Isadore Twersky. The Dihle course and Helmut's influence led me to take or audit several more courses from Zeph Stewart. [Maybe I should confess a sin here. In those times it was difficult for a HDS non-classics student to get a key to the Classics Library in Widener, but somehow I managed. The key was to be returned, but I still have it; the last time I was in Widener, it still worked!] These were exceedingly challenging experiences, but I remain grateful to this day for what I learned in the process.

I also profited greatly from Helmut's lectures on Paul and on Hebrews as well as discussion with him on these topics. To this day I primarily teach Pauline studies, which is a reflection in part of Helmut's influence on my interests and passions.

I so enjoyed conversations that Helmut and I, an identifiable "conservative" student, had on various issues. I recall our sitting together on a bench in the little plaza outside the library; Helmut asked me why the gospel writers never put a word in Jesus' mouth about circumcision. Before I could respond, he said: "And do not tell me it is because the gospels accurately reflect what Jesus said!" Another time Helmut asked me how a scholar as great as Hans von Campenhausen could argue that the tomb [of Jesus] was empty; my attempted response led Helmut to conclude that I was a "hopeless" conservative. One of our lasting main disagreements concerns the status of 1 Thessalonians 2:13-16; the issues still plague and intrigue me, and I regret that I have never written an article on this passage. But, what is so wonderful is that over these forty-two years that we have known each other, I have never felt any disrespect from Helmut for me, my scholarship or my commitments. And, I remain deeply respectful of him and his commitments.

Helmut always challenged me in good ways in my doctoral work. I loved the exegetical task, and Helmut pressed me to be more thorough and searching than I had ever been. I took a full-time teaching position before I finished my dissertation; I think Helmut feared I would never finish. But he never abandoned me; the look of joy on his face when I finished my dissertation oral examination and his words "We should have hired a band!" still encourage me to this day. Although Second Temple Judaism never seemed to be high on Helmut's list of concerns, he took a keen interest in my dissertation, which dealt with the Hebrew Bible/LXX and Second Temple Jewish literature.

Part of my enthusiasm for and gratitude to Helmut as a mentor led me to recommend that many of my own students go to Harvard to study with him. They are represented in this volume by Chris Matthews.

My last resident year at Harvard, 1968–1969, was, of course, famous for the student unrest and protests on campus. I think that this was a difficult time for all faculty, including Helmut. Students published at that time their first "underground" evaluation book of professors. Some unkind (and unfair in my judgment) things were said about Helmut. As one of his "senior" students I went to him (perhaps presumptuously on my part) to counsel him not to respond. I recall one day in a class when a University "radical" student walked in and went to the podium and pushed Helmut aside, declaring that it was his turn to speak. I sensed that Helmut was seething and perhaps unsure as to what to do. As the senior student in the room, I stood up and declared that class was dismissed for the day, asked another student to call security and then went to be with Helmut. I loved him and did not want him hurt or abused in any way.

I learned important personal lessons from Helmut, too. From both Helmut and Gisela my wife Jeannette and I learned the importance of extending care and hospitality to students, which we have emulated over the years. I recall with special pleasure a December 31st in their home when the four of us held hands and prayed as the New Year arrived. In addition, I admire Helmut's commitment to the church, which is, in my opinion, very important for teachers of the New Testament. And, in these last four years of my personal struggle with incurable cancer, Helmut and Gisela have remained friends who express care and prayer.

In summary, like all of my colleagues, I owe much to Helmut, both academically and personally. It is wonderful to still count Helmut and Gisela as friends now forty-two years after we first met.

—*David Scholer*

T HOSE OF us who studied with Professor Koester soon after he was appointed to the Harvard faculty at a young age have received remarkable benefits for several decades. Not only were he, his wife Gisela, and
their family hospitable to us while we were students, but those of us who
are completing long academic careers can now recognize that our debts to
the Koesters have accrued throughout our professional and personal lives.
It is a privilege to be given this opportunity for expressing our gratitude.
The theme of personal appreciation will return briefly in the conclusion,
but the focus of these words will be on a rich and complex relationship
with Professor Koester as an internationally recognized scholar, an atten-
tive and demanding doctoral supervisor, and an exemplar and mentor in
his continued growth, discipline, and public contribution.

Four of us entered the Harvard doctoral program in New Testament
and Christian Origins together in 1966: Robert Karris, Pheme Perkins,
Sam K. Williams, and I. All of us had come with considerable awe for
Harvard's remarkable New Testament faculty. Watching the department
clean house of graduate students who had been in residence for years,
with declining prospects for completion, put the fear of the Lord (or
maybe of the faculty) in us. We formed a pact in our first year to read together, challenge one another, and survive together, if we could. Professor
Koester was a major reason we all made it.

The New Testament Seminar was our ordeal. Professor Koester
chaired our first seminar on the shorter Pauline writings. Some of the
experienced doctoral students tried to help us figure out how to write
something that would be more than cannon fodder for all the faculty
and graduate students gathered on Monday afternoons. Our terror was
only exceeded by our ignorance. In analyzing a pre-Pauline hymn, one
of our number, not faring too well in defense of his paper, took a stand,
"Well, my analysis *could* be right!" The silence was deafening, broken by
Professor Koester's quip, "Of course anything is *possible*. You could even
see a horse vomit." Back we all went to the library!

The Seminar, however, was also the place where we watched the
faculty and those writing dissertations talk to each other and heard how

the arguments work. In these years, Professor Koester was constructing his analytical essays that were later collected in the volume with James Robinson on *Trajectories through Early Christianity*. Faculty and smart teaching fellows like John Gager, Sheldon Isenberg, and Richard Horsley would take each other on with even more vigor than was expended on first year scapegoats. With all respect, Professors Strugnell, Stendahl, Hartman, MacRae, and Georgi engaged Professor Koester's arguments at levels we could barely plumb. The Seminar taught us to be prepared and unafraid when we saw fierce discussions in scholarly debates. And when we read the texts from Second Temple Judaism with Professors Stendahl and Strugnell, Professor Koester and his colleagues were right there again with intense discussions of method and content. The fear soon gave way to exhilaration, even courage.

My own greatest scholarly debt to Professor Koester lies somewhere in the arena of his capacity to welcome interpretation that complicated the "trajectories" of his work. Serving as his teaching fellow in 1969–1970, I was engaged in seeking to explicate "the ecclesiological implications" of the Christologies of his essay "One Jesus and Four Primitive Gospels" (*HTR* 61 [1968]). I observed the fecundity of his analysis in his lectures and teaching to the point that I used this essay for many years in my own teaching on the canonical gospels and "the crucible of Christianity." Still, after several months of seeking to explore the understanding and practice of the communities growing around Jesus as "divine man," I was unhappy with the meager results. In one of several wild and stimulating conversations with Dick Horsley, we agreed that the question needed to be turned around. In many ways, we learned this from Professor Koester. The question was not what communities did the varied Christologies produce, as if it were a question of the history of ideas producing institutions. But in what communities and social contexts were the stories of Jesus as wonder worker most plausible and powerful?

Without Professor Koester's seminal work on "four primitive gospels," my inquiry into the "divine man" would not have been possible. Without his capacity at least to entertain a proposal that challenged some of the assumptions of his analysis, my dissertation on *The Charismatic Figure as Miracle Worker* would have been dead on arrival. There was an awkward moment in the thesis defense when Professor Georgi noted that although I had benefited from his work on 2 Corinthians, I disagreed at points. Then he added, "You also disagree with Helmut," and he pushed on the tender spots. Every graduate student fears that moment. Blessed be Professor Koester's *savoir faire*. I don't know to this day what he made of the occasion, but he got my project published.

The late 1960s were a difficult time at Harvard University, because the agonies in the soul of the nation were visited upon the academy. Harvard Divinity School struggled with the question of whether to accept funds from the Rockefeller family for a residence hall, and Dean Stendahl, the faculty, the students, and the constituents were divided. In the context of the protests against the Viet Nam war, it seemed to be an apocalyptic time with "father" set "against son and son against father, and mother against daughter and daughter against mother" (Luke 12:53—my friends knew I would need a text from Luke). It was a fierce time for junior faculty and teaching fellows in their relations to senior faculty, and Professor Koester was in the midst of the struggle. Having observed the politicization of European universities, Professor Koester sought to establish a bond with students to help carry the "HDS Community" through. Although that strategy was not very successful given the suspicion and righteousness (on every side) of the time, these were precisely the months in which my dissertation project was reviewed and approved. The lesson which I carried from Professor Koester throughout my academic life, especially through eighteen years as a seminary president, was the necessity of protecting the life of academic freedom: *die Gedanken sind frei*, even in the midst of university politics.

But we also learned much sweeter lessons from Professor Koester, especially as a teacher, a scholar who continues to learn, and a whole human being.

Watching him as a teacher with the M.Div. and M.A. students at HDS was instructive for all who would spend their lifetimes in a college or seminary classroom. Doctoral students are susceptible to infections of arrogance, and some doctoral supervisors abet the disease to the harm of their students. Professor Koester was not one of those who wished the Divinity School would be absorbed into the Graduate School of Arts and

Sciences. He knew the quality of the New Testament doctoral program owed no apology, but he also saw that the vocation of HDS required disciplined attention to the work of those who were pursing professional degrees. His students of every decade report that he gave himself to them, attended to their learning, and respected the vocations in communities of faith or other publics where they would be called to lead. The care he invested in his Divinity School lectures and the hospitality he and his wife Gisela gave to all his students remain inspiring.

Having invested most of this statement in words of appreciation for Professor Koester's early impact on many of us, it will be important to hear the ways others pay attention to how his scholarship grew and changed to the benefit of later generations. None of us in those early years would have predicted his amazing interest in archaeology and the material culture of early Christianity. His grasp of the pre-canonical traditions was already evident, including his interest in their enduring impact on Christian diversity, but who would have imagined the elegance with which he drew in the complexities of formative Judaism and the information from non-literary sources and excavations? Reading his accounts of *The History and Literature of Early Christianity* has been a veritable renewal of the rich discussions of the New Testament Seminar. Professor Koester has continued to be our teacher and mentor.

The last word, however, is both German and Yiddish: *Mensch.* Professor Koester is a man who was a prisoner of war in his youth, a brilliant student of Rudolf Bultmann, a *Wunderkind* at Harvard, a faithful leader with Gisela and their family at University Lutheran Church, a musician, and a friend. Whatever accolades he receives, one is evident to all who know him: "He married well." He and Gisela hosted generations of students in their home and visited many former students. Gisela can even be credited with rescuing our niece when she fell into deep water at our northern Minnesota cottage.

As Professor Koester (I still can't quite call him Helmut, in spite of direct instructions from him as early as 1968) turns eighty, my wife

Martha and I are grateful to join the chorus of those expressing thanks to the Koesters and gratitude to God for them.

In good faith,

—David L. Tiede

Harold W. Attridge

It has been more than thirty-five years since, as a fledgling Ph.D. student, I first encountered Helmut Koester, one of the distinguished senior professors at Harvard. Several things struck me then about his approach to the enterprise of New Testament scholarship and they have continued to impress me throughout the years that followed.

His vision of the field was breathtaking. He was then and, I believe, now remains convinced that to have even a rudimentary understanding of the New Testament, one has to know its context and know it well. The interpreter of the New Testament, that is, has to understand what was happening in the world of Hellenistic philosophy, Roman social history, the Jewish encounter with Hellenism, and also should be familiar with the developments in the early history of Christianity that realized the varied potential of the earliest Christian movement. The scholarship that Helmut produced in the intervening years has given substantial form to that vision of the field, from his seminal essays, with his friend Jim Robinson, on trajectories in early Christianity, through his introduction to the New Testament, to his study of early Christian gospel literature, he has embodied an encompassing scholarly vision.

Helmut's scholarship has been marked by the combination of rigorous learning and penetrating insight that is hallmark of the finest of humanistic and theological learning. While firmly rooted in the best traditions of traditional New Testament scholarship, Helmut has also been willing to explore new areas seldom engaged by members of the guild. His passionate engagement with the archaeological study of the Aegean has inspired a generation of students of Christian origins to take seriously the material culture within which Christian communities took shape and to which they responded. I have not had the pleasure to accompany him on one of his archaeological expeditions, but I understand that he still sets the pace for budding scholars many years his junior. The remarkable energy of Helmut in the field is continuous with the energy that he has always displayed in his scholarly pursuits.

Another hallmark of Helmut's scholarship has been its profound theological commitment. The precise form of his synthesis of history and

40

theology is something with which I have wrestled over the years and I am not sure that I would articulate their connection in the way that Helmut does. Nonetheless, his insistence that theology and historical study are in a fruitful dialectical relationship is a vision that I wholeheartedly share. It has been particularly meaningful to me as I have engaged over the years ever more in depth with the project of theological education.

While dedicated to his own research, Helmut has also played a major role in the leadership of the scholarly community. As an officer of the Society of Biblical Literature and one of the leaders of its transformation into the modern scholarly society that it is, he has been unstinting of his time and energy in support of the development of biblical scholarship generally. Beyond his involvement with the SBL his most significant act of leadership has no doubt been his role on the editorial board of the *Hermeneia* commentary series, a project in which I have had the privilege to participate for the last fifteen years. As a leader in the field, devoted to the welfare of the discipline and to his many students who engage in it, Helmut is a model for all of dedication for all of us who have benefited from his engagement with our own work.

It has been my privilege to know and to work with many leading scholars during the last thirty-five years. Helmut Koester will always stand in the forefront of that great cloud of witnesses who inspire by word and deed.

—*Harry Attridge*

O N A February afternoon in 1970 I (then a Middler at ETS) slipped into a seat at HDS for a Seminar entitled something like "Gospel Traditions in the Early Church," taught by one Helmut Koester, about whom dire warnings had been issued. That semester was no languid amble through the halcyon groves of Academe: it exploded with the invasion of Cambodia. At the time it seemed utterly unremarkable that, after class one afternoon, another student and I walked, briefcases in hand, to Harvard Square and headed for downtown Boston and a demonstration against the Chicago Seven verdict. After participating in obligatory ritual chants ("POWer to the PEOple, POWWWER to the peoPLE"), evading some bricks, and observing efforts to provoke the police, we returned a few hours later, discussing shop on the crowded train. *Apophthegm:* On a later occasion, when Koester and Georgi had taken me to dinner at the Faculty Club and I was bewailing the war in Vietnam Helmut said: "You're always on the wrong side." This observation permanently banished my naïve American idealism.

That 1970 seminar changed my life. From the first day I was hooked by the subject and by the professor. He was not charismatic. The method was generally inductive. Papers were approached obliquely. I could not then and cannot now readily explain Koester's appeal. He did not motivate by exhortation or assurance. Perhaps it was his evident assumptions that one could do it . . . and who would want to do anything else? Koester taught us to do research and how to do research. I have never forgotten his little tips (such as using Y to mark LXX psalms in one's notes).

The bigger tips have also endured. Among these are: Don't stay off other people's property, for the boundaries that separate NT from Apostolic Fathers, Christian Apocrypha, and Patristic literature, Qumran from Philo, are often unhelpful; questions are more important than answers; learning how to pose the appropriate questions is crucial; cultivate a primary method, but don't let it own you; exercise methodological rigor while maintaining the understanding of method as means, not end. To promulgate these values would have been trite. Part of the enchantment of that seminar was the experience of seeing an expert grapple with the material rather than magically unravel complexities. If form criticism does nothing else, it teaches one to develop a good eye.

The next Seminar was the Fall 1972 NT Doctoral Seminar. That inaugurated the Koester revolution: archaeology as subject and untraditional format. The quantity and quality of the work generated that term amazed those who participated in it or who later reviewed the bound volume. When asked by others how he had got us to produce, I had no good answer, but I knew that I loved it at the time, as did we all. The only rival was Dieter Georgi's Seminar on Mysteries and Sacraments, which had probably inspired Helmut to set aside his former style.

Not to engage in invidious comparison: Georgi taught us how to think through his less direct, more Socratic, fashion. Apples *can* be compared to oranges. George MacRae taught the importance of clarity in communication, the limits of speculation, and practicality. Set reasonable goals and meet them. John Strugnell taught us to view all solutions as limited, that assured results were a phantom. He was, in one sense, the "deconstructionist" of the department. The basis of his inspiration was *imitatio magistri*. Krister Stendahl invited graduate students to attend his lectures, which amounted to a graduate seminar in teaching undergraduates.

Whereby the foregoing is illustrated through example: An apophthegm. When asked by a student how much of Bultmann's *Geschichte der Synoptischen Tradition* would remain after a thorough revision, Koester replied, "About 80%." Whereupon Strugnell exclaimed, "Ah, Pietas!"

Codicil: in 1973 Koester said to me: "You don't make any progress in scholarship until you realize how *schtupid* your teachers were." True learning is dialectical, argument with one's teachers. Likewise, teachers honor their students by arguing with them. Authentic disciples do not simply repeat the words of their masters—which is not to say that they improve upon them. For good, bad, and indifferent examples of that process one may survey the history of the gospel tradition.

—*Richard I. Pervo*

The Koesteriad

TELL ME, O Muse, of the man of many methodologies, Helmeted Koester. Many were the people whose city he saw—Ephesus, Athens, Corinth, Delphi, and Philippi—and whose minds he learned—Bultmann, Conzelmann, and Bornkamm—and many the woes he suffered in his heart upon the sea, seeking to win knowledge on the sacred ship Hargo with his comrades Saint George MacRae, Herr Dieter Georgi, and Sir John Strugnell. It was my good fortune to travel on the Hargo for a great voyage before Helmeted Koester launched out on other adventures with the champions Queen Elizabeth, Fr. Bovon, and King Karen. With us sailed many others who tell their own stories of adventures in this book.

Together we set sail over the treacherous waters of the study of antiquity to learn the wisdom of the dead: the apostle Paul and the authors of Q, Mark, Matthew, Luke, and John, among many others. Helmeted Koester was a fit pilot for the craft by dint of his brilliance, erudition, unbending dedication to the task, good humor, loyalty to his comrades, astonishing energy, and enormous curiosity for things arcane. Each week he met with his crew (the HDS New Testament faculty and students) to chart our journey. These meetings not only provided guidance for our ship but reinforced the impression that our voyage was important not just for historical or religious knowledge but for the transformation of culture. It was here that we learned that our quest was a communal one, and each of us used distinctive skills for the benefit of all.

The skills of Helmeted Koester and the rest of his crew were necessary because of the enormous distances between ourselves and the land of the dead; many were the dangers and many the temptations along the way. We sailed past the Sirens of more lucrative routes, we avoided the Skylla of eisegesis, escaped the one-eyed Cyclops of religious intolerance, sailed past the Clashing Rocks of faculty politics, and we deaf to the Sirens of historical positivism and the Griesbach Hypothesis.

When we arrived safely at the land of the dead, Helmeted Koester, Herr Dieter, Saint George, and Sir John conjured forth the dead with a magical brew of historical criticism, form criticism, source criticism, redaction criticism, and linguistic and literary analysis. In the darkness, the shades of the dead slowly gathered to reveal their secrets: the once-blinded seer Paul of Tarsus, the anonymous authors behind the gospels, including the author of the Gospel of Mark who wanted to meet us, "and immediately." Matthew's Peter gave us the keys to the kingdom, and we were allowed to enter even deeper regions of the land of the dead. Here we also encountered Philo, Josephus, the authors of many Jewish pseudepi-graphical works, the Clements of Rome and Alexandria, Ignatius, Justin Martyr, Tertullian, Origen, and the creators of many apocryphal gospels, acts, epistles, and apocalypses, including many Gnostics. Each of them revealed his or her wisdom. Only the historical Jesus failed to be enticed by the allurements of our methodologies.

Once we accomplished our goal, Helmeted Koester piloted the sacred ship Hargo back through the dangers of the open sea on our *nostos* home and to his wise and faithful Gisela. Their home became a refuge to many of us, who remember fondly humble but gracious hospitality, stimulating conversations, much music making, and returning home with produce from their enormous garden and occasionally even baby clothes. It was in their home that we crew members knew that we were valued not only for the skills we brought for the voyage but also for our friendship.

For many of us, the adventures on the Hargo with Helmeted Koester and the other champions happened long ago in our youth, but we still recall that voyage with fondness and gratitude. Many of us have returned to the land of the dead on voyages of our own and used newer methods to conjure ancient authors to reveal their secrets, many of which differ from the secrets revealed to us long ago. Even so, these subsequent voyages would have been impossible if we had not learned from Helmeted Koester that such voyages, though potentially dangerous, are important and require dedication, energy, and wisdom. Danke, Kapitän Koester!

—*Dennis MacDonald*

I T WAS fall semester about 1971 or 1972 at HDS, the "Lower Seminar" on Wednesday afternoon from 3:00–5:00 p.m. The format was discussion of student papers that had been circulated previously. Helmut was the lead faculty member, and I had submitted one of the two papers that would be discussed that afternoon. As we were entering the room and settling into our places, Helmut approached me tentatively and asked: "Would you mind if I use your paper as an example of what *not* to do?" What could I say? "Oh yes, of course not," I murmured. When the seminar commenced, he did so for an hour. Since then, I have delighted to tell this story to incoming students in my seminars. I think it may give them hope!

Later in my program, I was researching the social history behind some of the Apostolic Fathers texts, one of Helmut's specialties, and in other texts of early Christianity. I was trying to learn what we could know about some of the names in texts like 1 Clement and Shepherd of Hermas, with respect to what we would now call their "social location." Helmut pointed out that there were identifiable slave/freedman names in the groups, because certain names were almost surely given only to slaves. I informed him that based on the prosopographic study I had done thus far, that was true in the first century but that by the early third century some of the same names were acceptable for freeborn persons as well, even those of fairly elevated status. With the slightly slumped shoulders of one whose bubble has been burst, he asked plaintively: "Even Fortunatus?" as if that might be one last holdout. Alas, I had to reply, "Even Fortunatus."

Still later in my program, when I had passed General Exams and was attempting to put together a dissertation under Helmut's direction, I turned in an admittedly poor first draft of a first chapter. When we met to discuss it, Helmut tore it apart for forty-five minutes. When he finally came up for air, I jumped in with: "Now say one positive thing about it." He laughed, thought a moment, and replied: "Well, I think you should keep working on it!" Eventually, with his guidance, a successful dissertation was completed.

I recall with gratitude the many social occasions with Helmut and Gisela at their house, and the ways in which they both welcomed us students into their lives. Telephoning Helmut at home, which he encouraged us to do, held its own challenges. The German custom of answering the telephone not with "hello" but with a low-voiced, solemn saying of one's name was a bit daunting. To an American unused to the custom, it sounded more like a growl than a greeting. But the warm and enthusiastic "*Ja, Lyn!*" that followed my self-identification made up for any initial doubts.

In 1981, a few years after I had (finally) finished at HDS in 1978, graduating with my Th.D. degree and dissertation on *Rich and Poor in the Shepherd of Hermas*, I was in Cambridge for a visit and Helmut invited me out for lunch. I naïvely assumed this was a purely social occasion. The question he put to me there took me completely by surprise: would I write the *Hermeneia* commentary on Hermas? I said yes on the spot and began collecting material for it, though I was not to begin writing it until 1991 and to finish it in 1998. Thus I had a long, if infrequent, relationship with Helmut as editor. He was always helpful, and—thanks be to God!—quite pleased with the results. The book appeared in 1999.

Much of my research interest has remained in the area of Apostolic Fathers and early Church, one of Helmut's great interests. I was his teaching assistant one year while at HDS, for his course in History of Early Christianity. I loved it, found his lectures fascinating, and was grateful for his allowing me to do one of them. His writings on the development of gospel traditions and other early Christian literature were guiding insights in my own thinking along the way. *Trajectories through Early Christianity*, his book co-authored with James M. Robinson, had just appeared when I was beginning my time at HDS. The notion of "trajectories" in early Christianity, an image borrowed from space travel in the Sputnik era, has remained a helpful metaphor for me.

The two-volume *Introduction to the New Testament* is a remarkable synthesis of Helmut's professorial career, a way of seeing the whole of early Christian literature as an organic development in many directions. While "trajectories" suggests linear movement, the alternative paradigm of "mind-mapping" might better describe this work. A mind-map is a diagram that starts with a central thought, word, or idea, then cognitively connects other concepts to that idea not in a linear way, but in multi-directional paths. There is even software available to chart such structures! Had *Introduction to the New Testament* been conceived and produced later in the technological era, it would surely have been helped by this analogy. Absent the technological angle, perhaps instead of a trajectory, the image of fireworks would be appropriate here: forces with different speeds and different colors branching off one from another and finding their own way to earth.

I was long out of student circles by the time Helmut began to develop his interest in archaeology, so was never fortunate to accompany him on one of the many research trips that he took with students. But his publications in this area, both image resources and essay collections on Philippi, Ephesos, and Pergamon, have been key resources for me as my own work has taken me many times with my own students to the lands and the very sites that he and his assistants so carefully studied and presented for the use of New Testament scholars and their students.

As Helmut has moved into semi-retirement, some things have remained, among them his characteristic bow tie and his refusal, up to last year and to this day as far as I know, to use email. Geography and work have usually taken me far from Cambridge, and we now meet only in passing at SBL annual meetings. Those formative years that I spent at HDS during my student years were under the influence of many great personalities who were on the faculty at the time. But primacy of place goes to Helmut Koester, whom I remember with gratitude as advisor, teacher, host, dissertation director, and editor.

—*Lyn Osiek*

"ARCHAEOLOGY CAN tell us nothing of substance about history. It is only the literary remains that give us solid data." This comment by a colleague at a recent scholarly forum took me aback. I thought we had all learned better. I thought that the Helmut Koester archaeological project had surely taken hold. To be sure, one should not overstate the contributions of archaeology, but neither should one discount them. That is why the Koester legacy of careful attention to the archaeological data using appropriate historical methodologies is so important.

What Koester had noticed early on was the loss of knowledge about and expertise in non-literary and archaeological data among scholars in New Testament and early Christian studies. Consequently scholars in early Christian studies were tending to overlook or misuse a large segment of primary material. Likewise scholars in Greek and Roman art and archaeology were missing out on the input of early Christian scholars. The research program Koester initiated set out to address this problem by introducing a new generation of scholars to the data and methodologies of archaeological research.

I was one of the early members of the project. In my first semester at Harvard, in the fall of 1972, I was introduced to the study of archaeology in Helmut Koester's New Testament seminar on archaeological sites in Greece. Each of us was assigned an ancient site for our research focus. I chose Delos—a rich site indeed. I had never had such fun in a research seminar. Indeed, my colleagues would probably say I had too much fun, especially those who remember the field trip I organized for the seminar to attend a special movie on Pompeii at the Boston Museum of Fine Arts. What a fiasco! How was I to know that it was a cheesy Hollywood production from the silent movie era about the last days of Pompeii?

Archaeology became my passion until the completion of my degree in 1980. In the fall of 1973, I joined Helmut's newly organized Research Team for the Study of the Religion and Culture of the Aegean in Early Christian Times. The team was engaged in a long-term project to gather a collection of resources for research into the world of the New Testament. In 1975, a group of us, under Helmut's leadership, went to Greece for a month-long tour to study and photograph the archaeological sites. Our goal was to put together a slide collection that could be made available to other scholars in the study of early Christianity, and, a few years later, our work and that of subsequent research team members finally resulted in the publication of the first collection of slides.

Traveling with Helmut was an adventure I will always remember fondly. We worked hard, but we had fun as well. For example, when we were at Delphi, several of us decided to run the length of the ancient stadium. Helmut positioned himself at the end to photograph us as we crossed the finish line. Though we started out in a friendly run, it quickly became a competition, one which I clearly remember winning (David Levenson and Tom Robinson both had bad knees; Lynne Landsberg and Natalie Petrochko sat this one out). But I have no evidence of my glorious victory because, when we reached the finish line, Helmut had to tell us rather sheepishly that he had run out of film and had not captured the moment for posterity. Fortunately, the majority of our photographs of the Greek sites were not required to be action shots.

It was during this trip that I finally got to visit in person the site that I had studied on paper for so long, Delos. However, there was a heated discussion among the group about how long we would stay in Delos. Helmut wanted us to divide our time between Delos and Santorini. Others of us argued for staying longer at Delos. Finally, it was decided that Helmut would go on to Santorini, the rest of us would stay on Delos, and we would all meet up later in Athens. It took me until the year 2000 finally to see Santorini; it was then that I realized why Helmut loved it so much. But Delos still remains my first love. The week-long idyll of the team there was priceless. We actually stayed on the island in makeshift quarters at the local café, and, most of the time, had the island to ourselves. This allowed us to study the ruins in great detail and imagine life in the ancient city.

Meanwhile, while we were being chaperoned in Greece by Helmut, Gisela was looking after our wives back in Cambridge (at least mine and Tom's; the others were not married). She invited them for dinner several times, continuing a tradition of the Koesters to entertain doctoral students frequently at their home. Their tradition of hospitality was remarkable and but one feature of the personal interest they took in the students and their families. To this day, Barbara and I are amazed and touched by how well Gisela and Helmut still remember and ask about our son, Adam, with whom they had actually had little personal contact since he was born just a year before we moved from Cambridge.

My first scholarly publication came out of my research team experience ("The Egyptian Cults at Corinth," *HTR* 70 [1977]: 201–31). During my graduate school years in the 70s, I also gained valuable field experience as an area supervisor at Caesarea Maritima in Israel, following up on recommendations by Helmut as well as G. Ernest Wright. My 1980 dissertation was on a subject that made liberal use of non-literary and archaeological data. My scholarly trajectory since then has continued in that vein as I have participated in various projects devoted to the study of the social history of the early Christian world and other aspects of Christian origins.

Today we are all familiar with scholarly works that are still filled with romanticized readings of archaeological data. Our colleagues in the guild continue to chase after specters such as the footsteps of Paul or the burial urns of the apostles. But the trajectory of scholarship that has been most affected either directly or indirectly by the leadership of Helmut Koester has insisted on a critical reading of the archaeological data, held to the same standards of scholarship that we would assume for studies in the primary literature of our field. We have learned that only a thick description of the world of early Christianity, in all its diversity and with all the specificity that might inhabit particular locales, can provide a sufficient context for understanding the New Testament and early Christian literature. Without that context, the literary texts are at risk of becoming artifacts without connection to a real world.

—*Dennis Smith*

The Seventies and Eighties

Helmut Koester in his Andover Library office

I AM NOW the age Helmut was when I came to Harvard to work with him. This puts me in a better position to see things from his perspective, but it also leaves me less directly connected to him, since we have not worked closely together in some time. I have heard hard words from some, whose experience of the man was less positive than mine, and I would not offend with an encomium overly idealistic. I am an idealist, but idealists do not always praise. Idealists whose ideals are dashed can be harsh and punitive. Though real enough to beg pardon from those I offend by lionizing the man, gratitude demands that I name the good—for I am one of many who have been gifted richly by being his student.

I am a biblical scholar engaged in the work of forming candidates for priesthood. Seminary formation involves working in an environment conducive to growth and development, and modeling as carefully as one can a life of growth and learning that will encourage the students toward a life of growth in integrity, and to the fullest possible extent, faithful and effective ministry. One cannot do this without a clear sense of the primary catalysts of development in one's own life both as a human being and as a professional; it is in this regard that gratitude demands that I say some things about Helmut's contribution to my formation as a scholar and seminary professor.

Many of the most important influences Helmut had on me, he would not have had apart from the work of his wife Gisela. I do not blur the distinction between the two, but it is simply a fact that I learned a great deal more about the life of a humane scholar by my contact with the two of them, than I would have with Helmut alone. They were not constantly together. Yet she was never far from him; he often referred to her or noted her point of view. But especially because Helmut and Gisela shared their table with students and advisees, Gisela was a part of our lives—a part of our access to him—and yet fully distinct and influential in her own right. She tutored us in German and shared stories of life in Germany. I was reminded of Gisela's importance to me a few years ago when, quite by coincidence, I met Gisela on a dance floor at a Methodist church in Belmont, Massachusetts, and we waltzed. How many people waltz with the spouse of their mentor fifteen years after graduation, I wondered. I knew she could waltz, because there were actually times when there was dancing at department parties in the 70s, and Gisela encouraged it. Celebrations like this have not recurred in my life as an academic [fade to: "Ballroom Dancing at the SBL/AAR Annual Meeting"].

I could write of things I learned from Helmut as a teacher, adviser, and scholar: the importance and excitement of the Greco-Roman world, the genius of the apostle Paul, the joy of textual criticism, and the interplay between rigorous scholarship and effective preaching. Yet what I most wish to address are the ways in which Helmut, by example and by direct instruction, instantiated in me the values of the modern humanist scholar, which the Jesuits had been working on with me in the eight years prior to graduate school. I will list these things in order of increasing importance.

(1) A humanist scholar has a store of knowledge beyond his or her area of specialization. Several times I heard Helmut say, "Don't be one of those scholars who knows everything about the discipline, but little about the greater world. In Germany at our comprehensive exams, one could be asked 'What direction would you be traveling, if you passed from the Atlantic Ocean to the Pacific through the Panama Canal?'" The answer is South or more accurately Southeast. Most of us looked it up before our general exams. I do not claim to have arrived at this broad range of knowledge, though I continue to strive for it, but Helmut did not just talk about it but manifest it in what he knew about music, geography, modern Greek culture, world literature, politics, international relations, photography (with camera and in the lab), and farming.

(2) More than once I heard him say: "In Europe nearly all the classically trained scholars play an instrument." He said it was not unusual when scholars were speaking of a new colleague to say, "Oh, and what is his or her instrument?" To hear Helmut play first violin in quartets with family members and some of my colleagues, and that we would have such music at departmental parties at his home, was an experience beyond my expectations of graduate study. I have delighted over the years in the rare joy of playing music together with students. It humanizes the learning situation. A humanist scholar also knows how to dance. This skill was

taught primarily by Gisela. Music and dance are essential to the liberal arts. I continue to strive to introduce them to students—but it's hard given the way things are arranged in academia.

(3) A humanist scholar is concerned about and active in engaging the problems of peace and justice in the world. Helmut's unhidden involvement in Amnesty International struck a chord with what the Jesuits had addressed in my prior education, and would address again in my year at Creighton University. He would speak about issues of justice as the texts called for them, and over drinks in Greece would enter the subject more directly. I cannot imagine what he has been going through during the last few presidential administrations.

(4) A humanist scholar is not contemptuous of technical acumen, nor reluctant to get his or her hands dirty with menial labor. The examples which come immediately to mind in this area are his skill as a dark room technician—which he managed to teach to some of us when we were working with black and white photos of archaeological remains—and his work as a suburban farmer. Nearly every arable inch of his Lexington, Massachusetts acreage was planted with potatoes, beans, tomatoes and any number of other crops, and charts were kept in his kitchen of kilos of each crop harvested in each year. Once or twice I recall him looking exhausted after an early frost nearly wiped out one crop or another and they were up late getting it all in.

(5) A real scholar does not need to distance himself or herself from the students. It took me a long time to get used to calling him Helmut—rather than "Professor" or "Reverend." A single anecdote illustrates his general attitude. Members of his Research Team (for Religion and Culture in NT Lands) had keys to his office, and we would often be in there working on the team's slide collections and bibliography. It was not a huge office. His desk abutted another desk in the middle of the room, which was for our use. Once someone else had arrived before me and was working at our desk, so I began to work at Helmut's desk. It was a time of day when he was usually in class. He burst in the room—books went in one direction, his coat in another, and I red-faced began to dive from the mentor's desk. He motioned abruptly and said, "No, don't get up. Keep working. I'm going soon." When he left the other person and I just

looked at each other. He treated us like colleagues, and we began to think of ourselves that way. It only became difficult much later.

(6) The last and most significant value that Helmut passed on to me, and to many others, involved his emphasis on table fellowship—and not simply as an issue in the early Church. Table fellowship was, and I suspect remains, incredibly important to Helmut, and I have heard so repeatedly over the years. All his advisees were invited to his home for dinner at least once a year. When traveling in Greece for the research program, group meals always included Helmut. Since this was the only graduate program I was a part of, I thought all graduate instructors did this. It is not easy to do. It makes demands on your home life, and leads to little jokes about your taste in furniture or dinnerware. This is the most important and the most enduring effect Helmut has had in my development as a human being and as a teacher. His preferred method of instruction was not the lecture hall, but around the table, and in certain cases, that table could become the place of a meal. I cannot separate entirely the exchanges of learning in the classroom and food around a table. It even enters my mind when at worship. It is one of the reasons I delight in teaching at an institution where faculty eat regularly with students—both in and outside of chapel.

How do you thank a man for such things? You only strive to pass them on, and you hope that he will know that in many of his students he has contributed to the spread of such radical ideals of humane scholarship. I strive to pass them on to my students. I am, we are, forever grateful.

—*John Clabeaux*

Helmut Koester was the first faculty member I encountered at the Harvard Divinity School. The occasion was the picnic for new students held on the lawn of the Dean's residence. I found myself sitting at a picnic table next to a Professor Koester. He asked me about my plans, and I explained that I was interested in New Testament studies but uncertain whether I would do an M.Div. or an M.T.S. When I indicated that after the Masters degree I planned to go to Germany for further study, Helmut responded with some vigor: "Why would you want to do that? We are all over here!" His pronouncement may have been a slight exaggeration at the time, but it was a prophecy fulfilled by the time I left Harvard with my Ph.D. in New Testament and Christian Origins. Helmut Koester and the people who studied with him played a crucial role both in shifting the field's center of gravity to the western side of the Atlantic and, more importantly, in redefining the field as something much broader than the study of the New Testament canon.

Koester offered many of us a direct link to the tradition of Bultmann, but he has been a major force in dramatically extending the scope of that academic tradition. With the help of my church's minister, I discovered form criticism in the summer after I graduated from high school. For me it was a means of taking seriously again the Christian traditions in which I had been raised. I began college as a physics major with a secondary interest in the study of religion. Under the tutelage of John Schutz, I came to see New Testament studies as the most "scientific" of the sub-disciplines within the study of religion. It had a clear method, form criticism, that seemed to offer objective results. The fact that the results of the new quest for the historical Jesus were rather meager did not bother me. Eventually I realized that the method is more art than science, but by that time I learned, mostly from Helmut Koester, that form criticism can be a powerful tool in many areas beyond the question of the historical Jesus.

Among the first things I read in my studies at Harvard were Koester's essays in *Trajectories through Early Christianity*. I have recently reread those essays in connection with some work on the Gospel of Mark, and I am struck by how well they stand the test of time, especially compared to many things that were written in that decade. Those essays reveal the range of Koester's creative extension of Bultmann's methods. Bultmann's studies of New Testament theology recognized the obvious differences among the writings of the New Testament, but his demythologizing program had a tendency to discover a single message of existential challenge beneath the surface differences and to discount texts that did not fit. By accepting the fundamental diversity of Christian traditions, Koester has been able to incorporate apocryphal texts alongside the canonical ones, without prejudice toward either group. Both groups are recognized as of equal value for reconstructing the complex history of early Christianity. As a result, his students have played a major role in renewing the study of early Christian literature outside of the canon.

The essays in *Trajectories* also stress the importance of the social dimension of early Christian literature. Koester places even greater emphasis than Bultmann had on the *Sitz im Leben der Gemeinde*, observing that not only particular units of tradition but genres of literature with their implied theologies survive only because they serve the needs of distinctive communities. Again, it is not accidental that many of his students have worked on aspects of the social history of early Christianity. Koester also followed Bultmann in placing the New Testament texts in the broader context of the history of religions. He simply extended the range of materials that are brought to bear on understanding the world in which early Christian literature was formed.

Koester's interest in the archaeology of the New Testament world was a natural outgrowth of interest in the historical and social contexts of early Christian literature. However, it was a move that was not obvious at the time and took some courage and commitment. The projects of Helmut's Research Team on New Testament Archaeology have greatly enriched the field of early Christian studies not to mention the lives of numerous individuals who have been given the opportunity to confront the artifacts directly and intensively on site. All of these lines of inquiry were, of course, brought together in Koester's *Introduction to the New Testament* and his subsequent articles to provide a broad foundation for further research.

For Koester, a commitment to historical research has never been incompatible with a faith stance or theological reflection. Because Christianity has been diverse from its very beginnings and has always been shaped by particular historical and social circumstances, historical study is a means of exploring faith. Koester has always encouraged his students to participate in communities of faith, whatever their tradition might be. He encouraged many of us to pursue the M.Div. degree, even though we were heading toward academic careers. An important aspect of the Research Team was taking slide shows out to the churches to share with them something of the New Testament world. Over the years that I was in Cambridge, Koester frequently commented on the pleasure he found in teaching Sunday School. Characteristically, his approach was to work with only a good translation of the Bible and an atlas, letting the participants explore the meaning of the texts in light of their original context.

Another important dimension of Koester's impact on the field was also prefigured in my first encounter with him at that picnic table, his genuine interest in students and colleagues as human beings. Over the years, he has made a point of inviting students into his home, of sharing the produce of his garden, and of making music with those who were so inclined and capable. For decades now Helmut and Gisela have been seen at every national meeting of the Society of Biblical Literature, stopping frequently to greet people, always inquiring about the development of family members and gardens as well as academic projects.

I, along with others, owe my understanding of our shared discipline to Helmut Koester more than any other teacher or scholar. I am glad to have the opportunity to express my gratitude for his guidance and friendship.

—*Rob Stoops*

IT WAS my honor to study under Professor Koester from 1976 to 1986, during which time Helmut coached and coaxed me through the M.T.S. and Th.D. programs and trained me as a copyeditor and managing editor of the *Harvard Theological Review*. Those who were fortunate enough to have Helmut Koester as Doctor Father stood tall indeed, having his shoulders upon which to stand. For me, a flood of memories accompanies the mention of his name. I am sure many will write of his whirlwind energy, his intensity, his penetrating gaze from across a seminar table, and his academic brilliance. Trying to catch Professor Koester in the hall between classes was somewhat akin to grabbing the wing of a low-flying airplane, yet he always managed to make time for individual students in his incredibly hectic schedule. In 1977 or 1978 Phil Sellew and I were given the opportunity to work with Helmut and George MacRae on the *HTR*, the *Harvard Theological Studies*, and *Harvard Dissertations in Religion*. Helmut had become editor of three publications that were years behind schedule and in debt. It was Professor Koester's task to get the publications on schedule and in the black without sacrificing quality. Phil and I, anxious to grab that low-flying plane, agreed to help get things on track. Into a small office we were taken and shown the nightmare that Professor Koester had inherited: on a table were several tall stacks of unread manuscripts. A lesser man would have despaired to fight such a beast, but Helmut Koester grabbed its horns and wrestled it to the ground.

In the years that followed, Professor Koester helped to breathe into me a crusading zeal for truth carried on by the community of scholars in their publications of books, journals, pictures, etc. During those years we fought to save many academic publications at Harvard from possible extinction, especially in the typesetting crisis of the late 70s and 80s. The route to the age of computers was a difficult one, and we were fortunate to have Helmut Koester as a captain to guide our ship through the rocky shoals. I was also fortunate to accompany Helmut on one of his trips to Greece. During the daytime we would visit archaeological sites and museums. Evenings we would often discuss academic topics at table. One evening I had too much ouzo and felt the effects the next morning. The next morning we were on a bus headed to Epidaurus and Helmut had taken a seat next to me. It was the only time I can remember wishing I was some place away from Helmut: as the bus swayed this way and that around the narrow, winding roads, I became very nauseous and had to ask Helmut to forgive my sickness and continue his discourse at a later time, which, to my relief, he did. [Perhaps it is improper, but I wish to take this opportunity to apologize to Professor Koester.]

I came to look upon Professor Koester not only as Doctor Father but as father. As a father, Professor Koester was an understanding counselor who trained so many to sit at the communal table of academics, and he hoped that I, too, would sit at that table and bring forth my own studies. It is not his fault that I came to serve that table rather than take a seat there. Tragedies in my life took me down a different path, but there, too, Professor Koester helped to guide me through a morass to drier ground. On my own, I never stood so tall as I did when I gazed from the heights of Helmut Koester's shoulders. With tears in my eyes and in true gratitude: Thank you, Helmut.

—Gary Bisbee

IT IS now thirty years since I met Helmut Koester, in the spring of 1976, my first year as an M.Div. student in Andover Hall. This course of study I thought would help prepare me for a career as a medievalist with a special interest in church history just prior to the Reformation. By the end of that semester I had realized with something of a happy jolt that I could concentrate instead on early Christianity and its environment, still serving my professional leanings as a nascent church historian while still cultivating my more personal interests in ancient Greek literature and culture. Helmut Koester was the major catalyst in that transfer of focus and academic interest from the late medieval world of Germany to the late antique world of the Mediterranean.

Since I arrived at HDS from Macalester College with an avocational Classics major to complement my more vocational History major, I was able to enter the Advanced Greek course as an M.Div. junior, reading Plutarch in the fall with Dieter Georgi, then Justin Martyr and Eusebius in the spring with Koester, a revelatory experience. A small point: one day I offered an observation on a text-critical problem in Justin's *Second Apology* (which then still lacked a usable edition) and Helmut immediately said, "Write it up and we will publish your idea as a note in the *Harvard Theological Review*." This was heady stuff, to have one's suggestions treated seriously, and also with a pragmatic twist (the fact that I never did write up the note is a possibly relevant codicil). Even more fun and enlightening was the course taught jointly that term by Koester with the classicist Zeph Stewart, where we studied the sources for the rise of Christianity within the Hellenistic and Roman world. Watching these two giants of erudition discuss topics like the Hellenistic ideology of philosopher kings, or Stoic notions of ethics, was exhilarating; having both scholars read our final essay exams was daunting. Though of course I would have liked to impress both specialists in their own fields, it seemed fair and just when Stewart commented that my remarks on Christianity were A level work, but my knowledge of the Greco-Roman material was closer to an A-. Koester evaluated the same essays exactly in the reverse! The pagan stuff I seemed to know well, but with the Christian data I needed more sophistication. So we were always pushed to improve, with praise typically spare and infrequent, and even then offered obliquely or with an equal or greater measure of criticism.

Though I had the great fortune to have Harvey Cox as my M.Div. advisor, I ended up taking most of my course work in the amazingly rich New Testament program. When Harvey protested at the start of my third semester that all four of my courses should not in all conscience be drawn from offerings in that one department, I was able to point out that none of the four classes involved studying a New Testament book! I remember instead reading an untranslated pagan philosopher in Graeca, the *Manual of Discipline* from Qumran in Hebrew with John Strugnell, the *Poimandres* from the Corpus Hermeticum with Georgi, and especially tackling "Non-Literary Evidence for the History of Religions in the Aegean in the Hellenistic and Roman Periods" in the "New Testament Seminar." In the end only one of my seven seminars in the department focused on a biblical text, and that ended up being the not-always so central Apocalypse of John. Personally I liked this disproportionate attention to the cultural world of Hellenism and second- or even third-century authors. Though all our teachers were committed to breadth of coverage, it was Koester who especially worked to put this "comparative" work not in the "background" but squarely in the foreground of our discipline.

We students of New Testament and Christian Origins had the remarkable privilege of being trained by the "Fab Five" set of Stendahl, Koester, Georgi, Strugnell, and MacRae. They all have meant a lot to me in various ways, and I could retail endless anecdotes about each person, whether funny, poignant, or both, but it is Helmut Koester that has meant the most for the longest period of time, from my M.Div. studies, then work as his assistant on the monumental *Introduction*, as part of the *HTR* team attempting to get it back on track, through writing of the dissertation, finding employment, his teaching as a distinguished visitor in my department at Minnesota, and beyond. Here I must limit myself to drawing three samples from that wealth of experiences.

One gesture has never left me. In my middler year at HDS I took the course co-taught by Helmut and Stanley Marrow of Weston on "Exegesis and Preaching." We were each to write a five-page paper on a specific pericope. I chose a very short text (Mark 4:10–12) but struggled might-ily to digest the massive secondary literature on the thorny issue of "why Jesus spoke in parables." I turned in a paper with more than four pages summarizing the contentious scholarship and less than a page attempt-ing tentatively to outline my own interpretation. I got my five pages back from Helmut at the close of the year with the grade "Incomplete" and the line "Come talk to me." His only advice was direct: reverse the proportions. Use no more than one page, preferably one paragraph, to set out the state of the question; use the other four-and-a-half pages to develop my own insights. Many professors I suspect would have simply made that comment when returning the original paper with a final grade, but what Helmut offered was the implicit notion that exploring my own views mattered. More than anything else it was this grant of a license to operate in biblical scholarship that counted; furthermore, this extremely busy man was willing to read and evaluate a second try and count that one for my grade. Over the summer I wrote something closer to the paper he wanted, and the theme returned as a chapter in my dissertation and ultimately appeared as an article in *New Testament Studies*.

Paradise and whiskey figure in my second sample. In the spring of 1979 I was (in addition to taking rigorous seminars on Platonism with our new teacher Margaret Miles and on Origen's *De principiis* with Brian Daley at Weston) immersed in Helmut's archaeology seminar. This would become his first formal course with students in Greece. It was an odd seminar in that the professor was away on sabbatical in Munich and Athens the entire semester, while his Teaching Fellow, the preternatural Holly Hendrix, ran the show in Andover Hall. My other main occupa-tion at the time was a seemingly endless attempt to finish amassing and pruning the bibliography for Helmut's *Einführung* for the delayed pub-lication of the original German edition. I was running or rather stagger-ing to the finish line, keeping Helmut at bay for a while with air-mailed updates. In return he let me know how anxious he was for the project to be finished and just how irritated he was with my delays; I think I sent the final entries just a week before departing Boston to join Helmut in Greece for our seminar travels.

Naturally I had some trepidation on the airplane winging to Athens that May as to how I would be received. My relief was both spiritual and physical when on the other side of customs there was Helmut with a big smile on his face, the greeting "Hello, friend," and the offer of a week's stay with him in Paradisos, a suburb of Athens where the Theological Faculty of the university kept a house for visitors. On the bus on the way to this 'paradise'—when my thoughts had rather been of hell or at best of purgatory—I offered a bottle of Scotch purchased duty-free on the plane as some sort of ritual atonement, and off we rode on a marvelous six-week adventure.

My final sample also features Scotch and delays in literary projects, though this time the time lag was a more of a mutual responsibility. I had been appointed to the University of Minnesota with the stipulation that I have my degree in hand, or more exactly, that I hand my dissertation to my advisor by September 15th. I beat that deadline by more than a week, giving a copy to Helmut over Labor Day in 1984, and then waited the entire fall semester in vain to hear his response. By January of 1985 my department had voted quite properly that I would be dismissed if I did not receive the degree in that (calendar) year. As it happened, Helmut was a guest in our home in St. Paul for nearly a week that same month while he gave a series of lectures at local colleges and churches. One evening, somewhat despairing of my situation, I took Helmut to our guest room and gave him the section of the dissertation he had yet to read along with another bottle of Scotch. As I remember the moment, my exact words to him were "Please don't leave this room until you finish at least one of these, preferably the dissertation!" I'm not sure that I said "please." Helmut's good humor and spirit kicked into gear, he gave me his advice, and I kept my job.

Many more memories push their way forward as I write these words, especially of evenings of music and laughter at Gisela and Helmut's table. Of these I will linger over only one: the historic and hilarious recreation of our advisor's doctoral examination twenty-five years before. With the entire department on hand, and Bentley Layton up from New Haven, the part of the ferocious Professor Dr. Benz was played by John Clabeaux, and that of Gisela herself by Holly Hendrix, with his masterful mimicry of her characteristic call of *Hel... MUT!* when his presence was required. I am honored to join my voice with so many of his students in repeating that call, now in praise and gratitude, with abiding affection and with deep, deep respect.

—*Philip Sellew*

WHAT A pleasure it is to join with others in offering this 'thank you' to our extraordinary teacher, Helmut Koester. It was the opportunity to study with him that first brought me to Harvard, as a Th.M. student, in 1976, and opened a new vision of early Christianity and critical scholarship.

The desire to attend HDS grew out of my reading of *Trajectories* the previous summer. That study was suggested by Robert Guelich, my New Testament professor at Bethel Seminary. He had studied with Leonhard Goppelt at Hamburg, and encouraged me to read Rudolf Bultmann and Walter Bauer, and then Helmut's development of this German scholarly tradition. In a volume soon filled with yellow highlighting, "GNOMOI DIAPHOROI" was especially insightful, bridging and integrating the traditional disciplines of New Testament studies and Church History in a fascinating way.

I initially wondered if a scholar of Helmut's stature would have any time for a "one year wonder" Th.M. student. When I wrote ahead to ask if he'd be my advisor, the prompt reply was warm and invited a personal meeting when we arrived in Cambridge. Throughout that year I benefited immensely from his guidance and embodiment of single-minded study.

Helmut wasn't shy in pointing me toward particular classes and colleagues. He had exacting standards and readily communicated a sense of how things ought to be done. In recommending coursework with Dieter Georgi and George MacRae, he praised their expertise and suggested ways their insights could contribute to my growth. I should particularly learn more about Gnosticism from Father MacRae, whom I soon thought of as "The Thunder, Perfect Mind." On a different note, when sometime later Helmut teamed up with Harvey Cox to offer "Heresies Ancient and Modern," I was intrigued by the chemistry between them and applied methodologies from their respective disciplines.

Taking the Early Christian Literature course from Helmut was truly unforgettable. His survey of the ante-Nicene writings was like a personal tour and his knowledge was simply encyclopedic. He loved what he did!

Discussions of literary genre, the transmission of manuscripts and growth of the tradition set the stage for my future studies. Today, I wonder if that was the final time he offered the course, as his interest in archaeological evidences was claiming increased attention.

After my Th.M. year, there was a break from degree work as I became pastor of a small Baptist congregation in the Dorchester section of Boston. Subsequently, with that church's encouragement, I applied for and was admitted to the Th.D. program in Church History.

By this time, a second mentor had emerged, George Huntston Williams. His "reminiscences," covering the entire sweep of the Church's story, built on and complemented insights from Helmut. Studying with these two remarkable scholars was a tremendous privilege. They were very different in personality and approach (after General Exams I characterized them as microscope and telescope). Sharing their company and watching their interaction with each other—challenging, sometimes exasperating, yet respectful—helped me reflect on the type of scholar I wanted to become. My wife Linda and I remember well sitting with Helmut at the Harvard Faculty Club dinner marking George's 80th birthday in 1994, and sharing personal reflections.

When Professor Williams retired at the then-mandatory age of 65, the study of "Old World" church history at Harvard underwent a major change. There was some discussion of whether the department, or even the discipline, should be continued. This shift occurred as I was looking past my "Generals," and anticipating the dissertation stage. Subsequently, working with newer faculty like Clarissa Atkinson, and especially Margaret Miles, proved a tremendous blessing. Nonetheless, there was no substitute for the Winn Professor of Ecclesiastical History agreeing to be my dissertation advisor.

I remember an afternoon discussion in Helmut's office, buried in the main floor Andover Harvard Library stacks. A look at the shelf of dissertations downstairs had revealed some huge tomes. How long should my manuscript be? His response (after clearing a chair by moving boxes of slides) was perfect: "The only thing that matters is if you have anything to say. If you don't, why bother? If you do, I'll help you any way that I can." That crisp word and promise was what I needed most. Several years later, following my dissertation defense, he invited me out for lunch. When I asked if he had the time (propelled in a hundred different directions), Helmut paused and responded that this was an old tradition . . . "and now you are a part of it." What an exhilarating feeling!

An early draft of my dissertation still bears the marks of Helmut's corrective hand, ranging from questions of interpretation to Greek accents. Writing on the Ignatian Long Recension, there was also opportunity to hear him reflect with appreciation on the work of the nineteenth-century scholars like Theodor Zahn and J. B. Lightfoot. It was yet another reminder of his vast knowledge of "the literature." I remarked that he didn't always speak so positively of English scholarship. Then he laughed and shared an Arthur Darby Nock story, in which the eccentric Harvard classicist had, during a seminar years earlier, retrieved from memory the occurrences of a Greek term the presenter had missed.

One of the greatest gifts Helmut cultivated (*insisted on*) was the ability to ask critical questions, particularly in the New Testament Seminar. Whether guiding discussion on the development of the gospel tradition, or asking probing questions of student papers presenting "Paul in the Second Century," everyone was kept on their toes—or heels or faces. In one session, a professor remarked that the text demonstrated an "alpha privative," but acoustics left several of us wondering what an "alpha primitive" might be, or look like. The New Testament faculty offered tremendous resources and Helmut was the driving force. At times I wondered if his queries and occasional barbs were merely rhetoric or academic sport. But throughout my studies, Helmut with dedication kept pushing the question: "What is your position and what's your evidence?" Serving as his Teaching Fellow meant interpreting Helmut and this critical approach to students in discussion sections. Recognizing 1 Thessalonians as among his favorite Pauline letters, I thought of 5:21—"Examine all manner of things, hold onto what is good." That remains one of my life principles to this day.

Whether through his research or remarks, Helmut sowed seed which became fruitful over time. In Kittel's *TDNT,* his *hypostasis* entry later gave rise to my "Faith as Substance or Surety?"—an article on the translation history of Hebrews 11:1. In a course lecture he observed that "Tertullian took Christian life seriously and made it impossible"—inspiring my further study of the North African who became a personal favorite. In his office: "Von Campenhausen is a great scholar, but on what basis could he believe Jesus physically rose from the dead?" Challenged, I turned to a renewed examination of the role of presuppositions (Hans' and Helmut's) in evaluating evidence for the Risen Christ. And the one who had repeatedly downplayed the species of "New Testament Introduction" masterfully redeemed the genre through producing his own. What else could find new life and relevance through a fresh approach?

Aware of the adventures of other colleagues, I wish that family and ministry responsibilities during HDS years had left room to join the Research Team on summer archaeological expeditions. When they didn't, he supported with understanding my "other" commitments, adding his own warm reflections about devotion to family and church. Over the years, different coasts, different ecclesial and theological circles, and an engagement with the whole of Church History (and Christian spirituality—sure to raise eyebrows) have led in other directions. Yet the debt is profound and lasting. Helmut, my life and my ministry as a pastor-teacher have been incredibly enriched by your onetime mentorship and continued influence. Thank you, happy birthday, and God's blessings to you and Gisela in the days ahead.

—*Jim Smith*

MICHAEL O'LAUGHLIN

I VISITED HARVARD Divinity School in 1979 and spoke to Professor Koester about doing a doctorate there. I was on a stopover en route from California to Great Britain to "Read Theology" at Oxford, which was a two-year commitment. When I told him I hoped to do a doctorate in Early Church History, he quickly (and humbly) suggested that I go to Yale and study under Bentley Layton. We talked more about the Harvard program, but I took his recommendation regarding Yale seriously. As it happened, Professor Layton was in England at that time completing a catalogue of Coptic manuscripts at the British Museum. I ended up seeing a lot of him while we both were in England; it was just long enough for him to find out that I had less Greek than was recommended(!). He thought I should do a preparatory year, like the Harvard Th.M., before entering the Yale doctoral program. When it was time to decide between Yale and Harvard, where I had been accepted without the extra year of remedial Greek, I chose Harvard, and Helmut Koester was a big factor in my decision-making process.

As I told Helmut when I arrived back in his office to do a doctorate under him, I considered it an honor to be admitted into the program and to be his student. Although the Harvard Church History faculty was rather under-populated at the time, the New Testament department was an all-star team, counting in its ranks Krister Stendahl, John Strugnell, Dieter Georgi and George MacRae, as well as Helmut Koester. With the exception of Professor MacRae, all were Europeans, and even MacRae had been trained in Europe. This reflected the traditional dominance of old-world, and especially German, scholars in the field of New Testament and Early Christianity. It was a happy coincidence that so many mature and accomplished scholars were assembled in one place; indeed, I felt like I had landed in the most high-powered NT department in the world. The weekly sessions of the NT Seminar were like scholarly summits, and this was a heady experience I will always remember.

I found Helmut to be a jocular, dynamic, and, yes, argumentative man with a lively mind. He could be both courteous and hard-headed, with an easy humor that softened the perception that he held to an ambi-

73

tious scholarly agenda. He was always ready for a laugh. I remember once the NT Seminar was focused on 1 Cor 14:16, where the Apostle Paul asks what some uninitiated person (an *idiōtēs*) would think upon hearing someone prophesying in tongues in the assembly. After twenty minutes of painful conjectures that produced no new solutions, Helmut voiced his frustration, "What were those *idiots* doing there anyway?" This was a typical Helmut joke.

His was certainly a dominant personality at the Divinity School; he was like a craggy *Übermensch* in a landscape dotted with special people. HDS was not all fun and games, and the New Testament field in particular is not for cowards. Here there are frequent earthquakes, seismic shifts, and researchers probably should wear hardhats and safety harnesses. In this uncertain and perilous atmosphere Helmut Koester was both comfortable and successful, ready to consider even earthshaking proposals with alacrity and always able to make sense of things afterwards.

Because of the speculative and revisionist nature of Koester's own research, it has not been universally accepted or understood. For example, his suggestion regarding the Synoptic Problem, i.e., that Matthew and Luke used an early version of Proto-Mark, and this Proto-Mark then became Secret Mark, which in turn became both Carpocratian and canonical Mark, is rejected out of hand by John Meier with the comment, "obviously, no serious sketch of the Jesus of history can use such material" (*A Radical Jew*, 1:122). For many, I am sure, Helmut's ideas were simply too conjectural.

My own reaction to Helmut's scholarship was quite different. Working my way through a field characterized by upheaval and contention, I came to regard Helmut's work, especially his *Introduction to the New Testament*, as an inspired but sober guide to the great debates of the day. Helmut had an extraordinary ability to sum up an issue and say something quite new and insightful without going overboard. I was not the only one who found Helmut's ability in this regard remarkable. I remember my fellow student Greg Riley's reaction to a piece written by Helmut on the Gospel of Thomas. "How can Helmut," he asked, "who does not know a *syllable* of Coptic, have *so much* insight?" Helmut's ability to put down carefully in writing a case that was both innovative and sanely persuasive was perhaps unique. Here is another example—I was trying years ago to get the gist of Kloppenborg's *rather* dry and detailed *The Formation of Q* and frankly I found it very difficult. In frustration I turned to the Q section of *Ancient Christian Gospels* and there Helmut had laid Kloppenborg's book out with beautiful clarity, as if with a sweep of his hand. That was what he did best.

In the twenty years since I received my degree and left the Harvard orbit I have focused on spirituality and psychology, and yet I still have found Helmut popping up in my life with some frequency. Here are some of my recent sightings:

On the day before I began this remembrance I picked up a book in German on the origins of Christian ministry. I randomly opened the book to a page on the Isis cult. The first words I read were: "*Helmut Köster sagt* mit Bezug auf den Hellenismus . . ." (Thomas Bonhoeffer, *Ursprung und Wesen der christlichen Seelsorge* [1985], 47). Here was a surprise—Evidently ministerial students in Germany must know their Isis, and so they had better know their Koester, too!

Here is another "Also sprach Helmut Köster": I was very gratified to note that our esteemed colleagues, the Sons of Q, credit Helmut with the first suggestions that the apocalyptic aspect of Q belonged to later redactions (John Kloppenborg, Stephen Patterson et al., *Q Thomas Reader* [1990], 22). The wisdom Jesus has been one of the most seminal and controversial ideas to emerge in the last decades, and I didn't realize it originated with Helmut. *Bravo maestro!*

Again, I recently used the PBS documentary, *From Jesus to Christ*, in a Christology class I was teaching, and I was struck that throughout that very useful film how much many of the scholars interviewed were Helmut's former students, and of course he was in the film himself. It was a good measure of how much influence he has had on the field.

Then there was the time, six months ago, when I took my family to a Cambridge restaurant. As we sat down I said to my wife, "This town never changes. It is so academic! Look at that guy over there. He looks exactly like Helmut Koester." And indeed, there was an eerie resemblance between my old teacher and the man at another table, who was even wearing a bow tie. Half an hour later my wife looked up and said, "Michael, it *is* Helmut Koester!" There he was, dining with James Robinson and Eldon Epp, just like the old days. We had stumbled on the *Hermeneia* board having dinner on their way to a meeting, and there was Helmut, his same ebullient, smiling self. He came over and greeted my family warmly, joking with my son that, as my *Doktorvater*, he was actually his grandfather!

I always felt fortunate that I had this German professor as my supervisor at Harvard. I remember the night I mentioned this to Helmut. We were at Dieter Georgi's house for a party, and I said to Helmut that having the two of them on the faculty made me feel like I was directly connected to the German scholarly tradition, and that was the next best thing to studying in Germany. Since 1819, when Edward Everett returned from Göttingen as the first American to earn a Ph.D., German biblical scholarship had had an enormous impact on Harvard, and Helmut Koester was for me a contemporary exemplar of the German influence and presence that has made Harvard one of the best places to study Christian Antiquity in the world.

I learned a great deal from Helmut, and I also tried to keep up my end by contributing a few jokes and wry observations. Since we were on opposite sides of the Protestant-Catholic divide, we ended up sparring about this every so often. Helmut's attitude toward Catholicism was ambivalent. He could sometimes be completely uncomprehending of the Catholic mentality, but then he would turn around and suggest that in some ways Catholicism and Lutheranism were almost identical. I honestly think he understood the Greek Orthodox in a way he could never grasp Roman Catholics. Yet let it be noted that another of my doctoral colleagues in Ethics, Stan Azaro, a Dominican priest, found the Koester household so congenial it became his home away from home.

Perhaps Helmut did not understand Catholics, but increasingly they were all around him. I teased him at one point that his beloved NT Department was becoming predominantly Catholic. He answered, "True, but they are all Lutherans in their minds." . . . Perhaps he should have said "Koesterians." And that is something that I think can be said of all of us: On the day I received my doctorate from HDS there were four *doctorandi* from the NT Department, one Protestant, one Catholic, one

Greek Orthodox and one Jew, but like so many in our field, we were all *Koesterians*, or perhaps I should say *Helmutians*, "in our minds."

Through his personal teaching, his scholarship and his *luminous* writing Helmut Koester has dramatically advanced the study of Early Christianity in America. He also formed a generation of American scholars. I predict that his legacy will be a long and grateful one.

—Michael O'Laughlin

STEPHEN J. PATTERSON

A *HARD-NOSED PIETY* ... Some years ago Helmut Koester published an
essay in the *Harvard Theological Review* (84 [1991] 353–72) titled:
"Writings and the Spirit: Authority and Politics in Ancient Christianity."
It is a broad, sweeping, historically rigorous piece, taking stock of such
diverse figures as Paul, Justin, Clement, and Origen—just the sort of *tour
de force* we have become accustomed to from our teacher. The thesis, in
a nutshell, is that early Christian writings originally were not understood
to be inspired by the Holy Spirit. Rather, they were created as political
documents designed to support and maintain the utopian communities
that were gathering in the name of Jesus in various places in the empire,
and to link these communities together in a common vision and understanding. The locus of spiritual activity for these early Christians was not
in their writings, but in the life of the communities themselves.

Koester begins with Paul's letters, arguing that they "are not witnesses of inspired communication and edification; rather, they are political instruments designed to organize and maintain the social fabric
and financial affairs of [the Pauline] communities" (357). This can be
seen both formally and materially: the letters are not personal letters, or
philosophical (as compared, say, to the Cynic epistles). Their primary
function is administrative, as Paul deals rhetorically with various issues
and problems that have arisen in the communities. The theological arguments that arise, he argues, "do not intend to serve any explicit spiritual
or religious purposes but to bolster the persuasive under girding of the
advice communicated in the letters. . . . The so-called theology of Paul's
letters must therefore be understood as secondary when compared to the
political intent of the letter" (358–59). And lest "political" here have
a negative, even cynical ring, one must realize that for Koester it does
not. Later he will make the striking claim, which those who studied at
Harvard in the early 80s will have also heard from Dieter Georgi, and
which is now heard of late in the work of Crossan, Horsley, and others, that Christianity was as much a political reality as it was "religious."
Commenting on the use of the very political term *ekklēsia* as a designa-
tion for early Christian communities, he writes:

> Christianity does not appear as a new religion but as a political utopia, the building of a new empire that was, like the Roman empire, understood as an alliance of cities. Constitutive were the assemblies of the people of each city, the local *ekklēsiai*, each held together by one bishop and one eucharist. The office of the one bishop in each city guarantees the integrity of the local assembly, and the church universal is thus seen as an alliance of the *ekklēsiai* of these cities—a concept analogous to that of the Roman empire as an alliance of cities. (361)

In this network the function of correspondence was similar to that of Roman officials: to foster relationships between local assemblies and to build unity. But unlike the correspondence that held the Roman Empire together, early Christian correspondence did not function in an authoritarian structure, issuing forth imperial edicts or conveying commands. Rather, it used the arts of persuasion, rhetoric, to create a network held together on the strength of shared values and a commitment to a more just form of community life.

Later Koester turns to the gospels with the same basic insight. They, too, "have been acclaimed in the later Christian churches as inspired documents. This claim, however, has no basis in their actual origin, composition, and usage" (366). To the contrary,

> The arguments of ancient church theologians for the acceptance of all four of these gospels were not based upon artificial proofs for their theological unity, not upon the evidence of their historical reliability, nor upon the claim that they were inspired writings, but on the tradition of their early usage in the process through which churches were maintained and developed. The building of the churches is again a political rather than a spiritual argument. (367–68)

As an instance of this political character, Koester cites the composition of Luke and Matthew. Both were attempts to bring together two quite disparate traditions, Q and Mark, with their very different theological orientations. "This combination," he writes, cannot be viewed primarily as a successful theological experiment; rather, it is an accomplishment of ecclesiastical politics. By incorporating the traditions of two very different Christian communities into one single document, both traditions were recognized as legitimate in spite of their theological disagreements. (367)

Whence, then, the idea of inspired texts, and a canon of texts whose value was defined by their status as divinely inspired words? Koester traces this notion to the Alexandrian school, with its roots in the Stoic method of reading revered texts such as Homer allegorically. Philo used this method to extract Platonic philosophy from the Hebrew scriptures, on the premise that God spoke through Moses and the prophets, encoding more than just the plain meaning in the text. Spiritual exegesis could extract from these writings hidden, spiritual truths—a notion later found applied to the words of Jesus in the Gospel of Thomas. Clement of Alexandria used the method on a variety of texts, both Jewish and pagan. But it was Origen who applied it to the gospels and to Paul's writings, according them for the first time a spiritual status on a par with the Hebrew scriptures themselves.

> All these writings now became the bearers of religious truths that were mysteriously hidden in the words of these writings and accessible only to the inspired interpreter. This implied that the apostles who had produced these writings were themselves inspired. . . . Because deep meaning could be found even in the smallest word of scripture, the doctrine of verbal inspiration of the entire scripture came into existence (p. 372).

I have rehearsed the main points of this essay here because it is illustrative of the most important thing I learned from Helmut Koester in my short time at Harvard and in the many years since: critical scholarship has purpose and meaning. Why write an essay that at first glance seems devoted simply to debunking the pious belief in divine inspiration? It is a topic hardly fitting a distinguished Harvard professor. I have never asked Koester why he wrote it. I frequently assign it because it addresses an issue that many of my students think is very important. But in this essay Koester uses the scholar's tools to break through a superficial piety about the text to reveal a deeper, more substantial level of meaningfulness. Koester is not simply a debunker. Here he shows that if you can brush aside the pious distraction of inspiration and ask in a more critical way about the genesis of these texts, you will come to a more important insight about the them: they were authored by people committed to building up communities devoted to a new vision of life lived out on new, non-authoritarian terms, in which there was to be no earthly lord, and no distinctions based on ethnicity, class, or gender. He ends the essay with these very high-fallutin' words:

> Liberation of the early Christian writings from their usage as inspired sources of doctrine and authoritarian control is the most dignified task of scriptural scholarship. Critical interpretation of these writings must recognize their original function: they are bearers of a story of salvation and witnesses to a political vision of a new ecumenical community. (372)

This, too, of course reveals a deep piety about the texts. But it is a hard-nosed piety that embraces the practice of critical scholarship and tough questioning with the clear conviction that new discoveries and new ideas are not to be feared. At the end of the day, Koester's brand of scholarship so often exposes our treasured notions as the mere treasure they really are, gathered only for moth and rust to consume. But that does not leave us the poorer for our work. There is a meaningfulness to history that allows us the pious expectation that the most rigorous historical-critical work will lead to new insights about life lived before God.

In my last few days at Harvard, before going west to continue my studies at Claremont, I had a conversation with a very good friend who was struggling through the doctoral program in New Testament. He had come to Harvard with very conservative views, but now felt himself bereft. Everything he had believed was in doubt, and deep depression consumed him. Turn back now, while you still have something left, he warned. Choose another field: law, business, anything but theology. Further critical study would only ruin my life as it had his. And so I stood at that difficult passage where many have stood. Old pieties beckoned me back to safer ground. But beckoning forward was Koester—the hard-smoking, hard-drinking, scholar with all the hard questions. Then, as now, the way forward looked a lot more interesting to me. It looked more like a real life. At a time when so much biblical scholarship appears to be content with tuck-pointing the tradition, letting the hard questions go for fear of the ruckus they might raise, Koester's way still beckons me forward into the fray. For this I am grateful, even today.

—*Steve Patterson*

I AM DEEPLY grateful for the opportunity to share in this venue the significant impact that Professor Helmut Koester has had not only on his discipline of New Testament studies, but also on his students, many of whom have made a considerable impact on this discipline as well and occupy important teaching posts around the world.

On a personal level, I have learned much from Helmut both inside and outside of the classroom. He was the primary reason I made the decision to go to Harvard Divinity School in the early 1980s. After reading his two-volume work *Introduction to the New Testament*, as well as his *Trajectories through Early Christianity* published with his longtime friend, James M. Robinson, I was convinced that I wanted to learn more from this man. I have been fortunate to spend many hours with him, not only in his office and in his classes, but also in his home as well as in various locations where professional scholars meet, and at the seminary where I serve.

There are very few professors in the world who could equal his contributions to New Testament studies. I have learned much from him and he has encouraged and guided me with uncommon wisdom and many acts of kindness in my own journey into biblical inquiry. He has also written letters of recommendation for me as well as a foreword to my own work on the biblical canon, which no doubt considerably aided in its sales! I remember one September day in his office how after discussing my interest in canon formation with Helmut, he asked me to consider writing on the criteria for canonicity. I later returned a paper to him that drew commendation as well as further guidance in the direction I was taking. In a very real way, Helmut launched me into my special canonical interests that have occupied much of my time and interest for the last twenty-five years. It is difficult to imagine the debt of gratitude one owes to a mentor who has given so much to me over the years.

Helmut's students know of his commitment to give them a hands-on experience in the places where the New Testament writings originated or were sent. Not long ago, on one of several visits that I have made to Greece, I met Helmut with a group of his students in the underground level of the St. Demetrios Church in Thessaloniki. I heard his voice before I saw him and had just mentioned to the tour group that I was leading that my former professor came here every other year! What a delightful surprise to connect with him there and subsequently at the archaeological museum in Thessaloniki, at Delphi, and later at Corinth!

Helmut set the standard for all New Testament introductions because he takes seriously the social context of early Christianity. Almost all writers of introductions today follow his example, including this writer. It is interesting that when my introduction was published, I sent a copy to Helmut knowing that he would disagree with several sections, but he graciously congratulated me on the volume. I reminded him that most of what he disagreed with was written by my colleague and not by me! He smiled and continued to show kindness and offer encouragement to me.

I was most pleased to host Helmut and his lovely wife Gisela here in Nova Scotia at Acadia Divinity College and the University. We invited him to give several lectures and afterwards engaged him in lengthy discussion with our students. On one of the afternoons just before we met with the students, Helmut told me that he wanted leave early for his hotel room for an afternoon rest prior to his evening lecture. He requested only a thirty-minute interaction with the students, but after thirty minutes when I interrupted him and offered to take him to his hotel room, he indicated that it was okay to continue with the students for a while longer. Forty-five minutes later I asked him if he wanted to go back to the hotel and he said that it was okay for him to stay with the students and quickly added that this was important! He was pleased with their interest in what he had to say and they were delighted to have a man of his stature and reputation with them. Need I say that he forgot about his nap that afternoon! I was impressed that this world-class scholar was willing to engage in conversation and interaction with master's level students and he even seemed to relish the moment! That was a good reminder to me that students are our primary mission and worthy recipients of our dedication and guidance. I might add that we held a luncheon for Helmut and Gisela with our faculty and he was every bit as engaging in his discussions with them as with the students and with his remarkable wit and comprehension of his subject.

Helmut Koester's areas of interest and influence have been wide-spread. He has an exceptional ability to grasp the basic context of early Christianity and the issues that most concerned the early followers of Jesus. He has made highly significant contributions to our understanding of the origin and reception of the canonical gospels and also the context of the early Christian church. Not many doctoral dissertations continue to have significant influence almost fifty years after they were written, but even today scholars continue to refer to Helmut's *Synoptische Überlieferung* as a standard resource for understanding the reception and influence of the gospels in early Christianity. Koester not only can examine the past critically, he also has the rare ability to look ahead and see the larger picture of his discipline without losing sight of the details that give rise to that picture. Perhaps he owes some of that ability to his *Doktorvater*, Rudolf Bultmann, who was known for being able to do the same.

If we are trying to survey Helmut's special interests, we must not forget his commitment to his church. Students are sometimes surprised to learn of the significant commitment and involvement that Helmut and Gisela Koester have to their church. Whether singing in the choir, playing his trumpet, or serving as an usher, teaching a Sunday School class, and even as chair of the trustees of his church, Helmut's commitment to the church is a model to all who teach biblical studies. While there are those who disagree with his interpretation of the New Testament, no one could doubt his commitment to the church. He is regularly invited to share with clergy in the New England states and elsewhere and occasionally preaches as opportunities arise. At Harvard, he and the chaplain of the University, Dr. Peter Gomes, have team taught classes that combined both exegesis and preaching, practical courses for those entering Christian ministry. While Helmut and I come from different Christian traditions, I have the utmost respect for his commitment to the church and its ministries. He has also been most affirming to those who are committed to the church's ministries. While he was in Halifax, he was invited to preach on a Sunday morning at a local church and he was received with heartfelt appreciation and deep respect.

At the time of this writing, Helmut Koester is just returning from Berlin, where he was presented with a richly deserved honorary doctorate. It is difficult to map the significant impact that Helmut has made on his many doctoral students, though one sees the number of his students who are household names in biblical studies today and are making significant contributions to New Testament studies and the context of early Christianity. There is also clear evidence that he has given sacrificially of his time and effort to make a difference in the lives of his students.

I count it a great privilege to acknowledge him as my mentor and friend and wish him God's richest blessings on the occasion of his 80th birthday! Thanks Helmut for all that you have done for me and for those of us who were privileged to be your students and are now your friends!

—*Lee McDonald*

T HE TASK is to prepare a lecture for a Biblical Archaeology Society audience. The topic is the account of Paul's visit to Philippi as told in Acts 16. The lecture will be delivered in a rather exotic location, but otherwise it has become a fairly commonplace activity. Study the text, outline an approach, choose images, put together a slide show, rarely time or reason for deeper reflection. This case is different, however, since it also serves as an opportunity to consider the many ways in which Helmut Koester has influenced my academic work and pedagogy.

The first folder I open is marked "Acts Reading" and dates back to my grad school days. It is filled with photocopies of articles dating from 1983 back to the early twentieth century. I am reminded that Helmut is truly a living link to some of the founding members of the guild of New Testament studies. Not only is he proud of knowing these figures, he always insists that we consider their work in our own investigations. He speaks with true affection of his days as a student in Germany, of conversations with Amos Wilder, Morton Smith, and other "Senior" colleagues, and I never saw him wear a bigger smile than when he was reading David Daube's "Question Mark?" poem to the NT seminar. Helmut is also willing to consider possible shortcomings of these legendary figures. When he led the Th.D. seminar in 1984, he selected the topic of how German theologians responded to the Third Reich. It could not have been an easy topic for him, but it proved to be a stimulating and enlightening experience for those of us in the class.

The fact that this will be an illustrated lecture can be traced back to the influence of all those hours spent in Andover Library. While the technology has changed dramatically, it is still often the case that a picture is worth a thousand words for bringing to life a site or a text. Helmut's great enthusiasm for flashing an image on the screen and talking about the details as if "you are there" continues to provide a model for using pictures as an essential aid in teaching. Of course it isn't the same without having to stop every third image in order to dislodge a slide jam in the projector. Our early attempts at slide duplication, including countless trips to Bob Slate in "The Square" for developing, seem almost comical today, when images can be copied, manipulated, and sent around the world in a manner of seconds. But the hours taken working with the slide collection and *ARNTS* was time very well spent, and it continues to reap benefits every time I look at an image of an ancient site or stand in front of a group and try to help them see the world that was.

While I enjoy the opportunity to lecture for the BAS, it is even more significant that this talk will be given on a study tour in northern Greece. The influence of Helmut Koester in this regard actually goes back to pre-Harvard days. In 1979, Diane and I first visited Greece as part of a St. Olaf College class led by Bill Poehlmann, who had been one of the very earliest students to travel with Helmut. Once after a particularly trying day with my own students in Nauplion, I wrote a postcard to Bill apologizing for any complaining I might have done during that trip. On several occasions, I have also written to Helmut and Gisela offering thanks for the example of not just talking to students about the ancient world, not only showing pictures, but doing the very hard work of organizing tours and taking the time to bring us face to face with the remains of that world. When I look at the faces of my students as they experience this same kind of insight for the first time, I am especially grateful to Helmut for blazing a trail to Greece and beyond.

During this trip we will also visit archaeologists in Greece, some of whom I met while traveling with "the Research Team." Helmut was far ahead of his time in seeking to break down boundaries between disciplines and learn from others what was important to them about a site. It is still surprising to some archaeologists that even though I study the New Testament, I am not seeking only the footsteps of Paul, or other evidence to confirm my beliefs. The rock reliefs on the cliffs above Philippi are more interesting than the purported "prison of Paul" found below. Helmut has consistently shown that the archaeological record offers glimpses into the whole of ancient society. It is that big picture, however fragmentary, which helps to make that world come alive and provides a chance for us to understand whatever text, artifact, or social phenomenon we are studying. Helmut not only models this pursuit of that larger view, but he also forms lasting relationships across disciplinary boundaries to help bring that view into focus.

Finally, as I look at this text from Acts, I realize that Helmut has also given me an appreciation for the "real people" behind this story. Not that Lydia, the slave-girl, and the jailer should be taken as real people, but rather they are meant to be recognizable characters whose words and actions make sense to the readers and hearers of the text. The author used these characters to convey certain images and ideas to the readers. This is why an appreciation for the material remains is so important to the Koester approach. If you don't understand the world in which these people lived, how can you possibly begin to understand the words that were written to them?

I will deliver this lecture on the island of Thassos, and the next day will lead the group on a tour of Philippi. It is likely that I would not be engaged in this work at all if it were not for Helmut Koester. His love of learning and his commitment to understanding the context of the early church is infectious. He seeks to share that love not only with his students, but also with audiences in churches and other settings around the world. In 1984, Helmut was kind enough to preach at my service of ordination. Among all of the friends and mentors who gathered on that occasion, it was especially important to have Helmut present. He also attended the vicinage council that met before the service to judge my fitness for ministry. As the council progressed, my unorthodox answers to doctrinal questions were clearly causing concern for some of the guest clergy. Then in the midst of my trial, I saw Helmut "sitting in the form of Paul," and I realized that Helmut "has come to look after me." He rose to speak and said, "I will save the tough questions for when Dan Schowalter defends his doctoral thesis." The room broke out in laughter, and I was able to survive my ordeal. Later on, Helmut announced that because he had been ordained by a bishop who was within the apostolic succession, I could now claim to be part of that august lineage as well. At the time, I was quite impressed with my new-found standing. Looking back at the last twenty plus years, however, I must confess that I am equally proud to be part of this "cloud of witnesses" as we pay tribute to the patience, guidance, and inspiration of our teacher.

—Dan Schowalter

CHRISTOPHER R. MATTHEWS

THE BUS is making very good time on the road from Argos to
Olympia. I'm sitting with Helmut in the seats directly in back of the
driver. Helmut's got the window and a better view than one wants of the
precipitous drops at the edge of the road, unobstructed by anything so
innovative as a guardrail. At lesser bends in the road Helmut explains that
the various shrines erected there offer tangible proof that some fortunate
soul survived after plunging from the safety of the road. We come to a
particularly sharp turn, grab our seats, and lean away from the window to
escape the onset of vertigo. There are no shrines in sight. We look at each
other and agree—no one leaving the road here survived! The bus driver
motors ahead unconcerned. Somehow he can see through the mass of
trinkets and totems hanging down across the large front windows of the
bus and so keeps both his eyes and the vehicle on the road. The danger
recedes and takes its place in memory.

Traveling across Greece in May of 1981 with Helmut's "Research
Team," looking forward to the start of my doctoral studies in the fall,
was a formative experience that has continued to have an effect on my
teaching to this day. As Helmut knew so well, nothing short of a time
machine could replace the practical knowledge of the ancients' society
and culture that one gained by walking through their physical spaces and
coming to an appropriate understanding of the scale of things. Strolling
across the agoras of Athens, Corinth, and elsewhere; standing within the
foundations of civic buildings and private houses; sitting in ancient the-
aters; taking in the plethora of ancient temples; all of this gave one an
indelible sense of the proportions of the Greco-Roman environment in
which early Christianity emerged. The contacts Helmut had established
with experts at many of the archaeological sites added immeasurably to
the comprehension of those of us who were neophytes. It was particularly
instructive to see firsthand the evidence of renovations carried out at the
turn of the eras to classical sacred buildings in Athens and elsewhere to
accommodate the cult of Roma and the various emperors. When I stood
on the balcony of my room at Delphi early one morning as fog drifted

90

through the mountains and ravines, I had no doubt at all that people had visions there and experienced the divine.

As special as the trip to Greece was, coming to Harvard was eye-opening in far greater ways for my own understanding of the origin of the New Testament and the history of the earliest church. Helmut was my advisor when I arrived and I had only just discovered his studies in *Trajectories,* which were fresh and exciting for me. His courses were dense with the kind of information and analysis I was hungry for, and it seemed almost impossible to find a limit to what one wanted to know and explore. Helmut's *Einführung* was in proofs at that point, so in some respects one might say he was at the top of his game on all matters of New Testament "introduction," a category that he greatly expanded to include significant attention to matters that were cursorily treated, if at all, by others as "background." This way of framing an approach to the New Testament quickly became part of my intellectual lifeblood as no doubt it has for all who have studied with him. And with respect to the New Testament itself, his article on apocryphal and canonical gospels, which appeared in *Harvard Theological Review* in 1980, reinforced the perspective championed in his introduction and opened up a lasting analytical perspective for me in the historical assessment of the development of early Christian literature.

It was my privilege to spend several years as an editorial assistant during Helmut's editorship of *HTR.* Publication was a bit backed up at that time, and the small group of us pushed hard to get out several years of the journal in about one year's time, including the triple-issue that comprised the Stendahl *Festschrift.* I still remember the great urgency to get the final pages to George Nickelsburg to meet our ultimate deadline of having the volume in hand for presentation at the SBL Annual Meeting. This was capped off by an after dark mad dash to Logan Airport to get the crucial package to the FedEx office to make the last flight of the evening.

The seminar for advanced New Testament students, the "afternoon seminar," still meets between 3 and 5 p.m. on Wednesdays. One of the nicest compliments I ever heard voiced by one colleague about another occurred in the wake of a particularly spirited session run by Dieter

Georgi. I had left the seminar with Helmut and went to his office to take care of some small matter of business. With the energy still swirling around from the rather heady meeting, Helmut reflected: "I wish I could do that." It was uttered with the utmost of fondness and respect for a colleague, and recalling it now, having lost Dieter, is all the more poignant.

All doctoral students of the New Testament and Christian origins at Harvard no doubt cultivate various oral traditions of their experiences in the dissertation seminar (or "upper seminar," for those hierarchically inclined). During my time this gathering took place on Wednesday nights between 8 and 10 p.m. (the "evening seminar"). Some of the stories generated by these assemblies are better left in the oral tradition! But I can relate two of my favorite anecdotes here in which Helmut delivered the punch line. I was not an eyewitness of the first episode, but the "tradition" was directly handed on to me by the "victim"; it clearly falls into the genre of "cautionary tale." As the story goes, after a difficult seminar session in which various faculty members tried their level best to help the struggling student arrive at a workable conception of his project, Helmut offered the final advice of the evening along these lines: "Yes, you can do that dissertation—but not here!" The second incident, which I witnessed myself, also centered on a student's attempt to define a viable project. But in this case there was a continual back-and-forth between the student and Helmut in which the student would simply not give ground to Helmut's critique. The evening culminated with Helmut explaining his own theological assessment of the topic under consideration, eliciting the following pronouncement from the student: "Helmut, you are dead wrong!" Helmut leaned back, folded his arms, smiled, and declared: "Prove that and you have a good dissertation!"

When my own plans for my dissertation were thwarted by the premature death of George MacRae, Helmut proposed a way for me to take my initial work on Acts 8 and extend it into a search of "Philip materials" over the first four or five centuries of the Christian era. To this day I wonder how some students get away with focusing on a single book (as I myself had originally hoped to do with Acts!) or even a delimited passage within a chapter of an epistle or a gospel for their dissertations. In any case, I finally managed to produce my own "trajectories" on the Philip tradition with the benefit of Helmut's oversight. In the very final stages of work on the thesis, as I neared a late summer deadline for submission for a November degree, I drove out to Lexington with a few pages of chapter four. I wanted to be sure that my several pages of engagement with three of Helmut's articles touching on issues connected with the farewell dialogues in the Fourth Gospel correctly represented his positions. Helmut was dressed in "full garden mode," and we appropriately paid homage to the healthy crop of vegetables growing by the side of the house before retiring indoors briefly to pull any weeds that might remain in my text.

There was so much to cultivate during those days at Harvard. The ideas and methods that took root there and grew robustly have served me well in all my endeavors since that time. Thanks, Helmut, for the major part you played in all this!

—Chris Matthews

THE HOTEL is . . . "inexpensive." We're somewhere in Greece. The travel alarm rings. For approximately three seconds, the electronic beeping is the only sound in the room. Then the John H. Morison Professor of Divinity and Winn Professor of Ecclesiastical History sits up in bed. Legs swing from under the covers, he strides across the room to turn off the alarm, and we're off.

The day's itinerary includes two to three dusty hours at an archaeological site. We took public transportation to get there, a city bus whose mechanical integrity was suspicious. Or was it five students to a taxi? Last night the archaeologist who excavated this site pried open two hours from her jammed schedule to meet with Professor Koester's students. She's done this in previous years and will gladly do so in the future. The student paper under discussion survived her scrutiny last night, but just barely. In the process she prepared us for the site, but not for the heat.

After the site visit there's a break for lunch followed by a museum visit in the afternoon. Then an optional climb up the hill to see the Byzantine church. It's not required for the seminar, just value added. Much to our chagrin, the John H. Morison Professor of Divinity and Winn Professor of Ecclesiastical History sets the pace, thirty years our senior and three paces ahead of the pack as we march up the hill.

***

How does one make a contribution in a discipline like New Testament studies? Many academic disciplines have a century or two of history to build on, but the study of earliest Christianity stretches back much further. Is there anything more to say, anything new to write? Of course there is, and many scholars contribute to that process. Sometimes the contributions have the character of refinements that enhance established conclusions, where new insights hone the work of those who've gone before. Occasionally, there are paradigm shifts, when scholars find a way to rearrange the arguments and evidence in order to move the discussion in new directions.

Helmut, however, has done something exceedingly rare during his career: he has shown us how to add a whole new range of data to the discipline. In his work Helmut has also made the more familiar contributions, honing insights and moving discussions in more profitable directions. But along with those achievements he also took on a fundamental challenge that others did not even see. What would happen if New Testament studies—traditionally a discipline devoted mostly to textual analysis—incorporated archaeological evidence into its research? What might the inscriptions, coins, architecture, and other material evidence from the Greco-Roman world teach us about religion and culture in Christianity's formative period? Indeed, what justification is there for studying early Christian texts without examining the *realia* from that same historical period?

For decades now Helmut has tirelessly pursued this agenda. He moved beyond the safer boundaries of his own discipline and learned another one. There have been regular seminars to Greece and Turkey that have introduced generations of teachers, researchers, and ministers to the excavated remains of the Aegean region. In order to make this possible there have been countless meetings and trips to build networks of colleagues in archaeology who understand the vision and the challenges. As a result, there are now dozens of specialists in early Christian literature who also engage the material culture of the early Roman Empire in their work, and dozens of field archaeologists anxious to engage in this interdisciplinary endeavor. It may well be that Helmut has created a new sub-discipline in the study of earliest Christianity.

***

After visiting the Byzantine Church, we hike back down the hill and there's finally time to freshen up. There is probably another meeting tonight with another archaeologist about another site. Or maybe it's just retsina and local fare, a long dinner at a restaurant on the harbor.

Much later that evening I ease into my bed, another long day behind us. The John H. Morison Professor of Divinity and Winn Professor of Ecclesiastical History sets his travel alarm.

—*Steve Friesen*

The Eighties, Nineties, and Beyond

Helmut as archaeological guide

I SHOULD NOTE at the outset that my doctorate was awarded by Boston University, not Harvard. During my Ph.D. program at BU, I took Helmut's New Testament Archaeology seminar through the Boston Theological Institute. That course—and subsequent interactions with Helmut and his students around the Ephesos, Pergamon and Corinth conferences, as well as involvement with the Archaeology of Religion in the Roman Empire group at SBL—fundamentally shaped my approach to the study of Christian origins. The invitation I received to contribute to this volume reflects my debt both to Helmut's intellectual generosity and, also, to his personal generosity. In addition to what he taught me in class, Helmut introduced me to a network of scholars he developed over decades of travel to Greece and Turkey. This level of academic generosity is usually reserved for a professor's own doctoral students; one would not expect it to cross the Charles River in Boston.

In the Winter of 1993 Helmut was teaching an extension course at the Center for Scriptural Studies in Charlestown, New Hampshire. On one of his trips to New Hampshire he telephoned me and asked if we could have dinner in Hanover. He said that he had something he wanted to talk to me about. On a very cold evening (the air temperature that night reached 25 degrees below zero), Helmut showed up in Hanover shivering in his VW bus with a warm greeting and an astute observation: "This bus was not made for these temperatures!" That evening, at the Ivy Grill (now Zin's) on the edge of Dartmouth's campus, Helmut invited me to present on Egyptian Religions at the Ephesos Symposium to be held on Harvard's campus in the spring of 1994. This invitation not only encouraged me as a young scholar, it also shaped my interests and historical methods.

I realize now, looking back, that Helmut was not only generous with what he knew, he was also generous with the people he knew: the Ephesos Symposium introduced me to a network of scholars that continues to enhance my work. In fact, my closest friends in the academy are former Harvard students with whom I have worked, traveled and played for over fifteen years. Many of those writing for this volume know that for over a decade Dan Schowalter, Christine Thomas, Steve Friesen, John Lanci and I have shared a suite at AAR/SBL. These relationships go back to the New Testament Archaeology seminar at HDS in 1987. But, they were crystallized through the Ephesos Symposium and my wife's (Marla) brilliant idea that we should share a suite at the Philadelphia meeting in November of 1995. This year's meeting in Washington will be twelve in a row. It will come as no surprise to those who know us best that Marla and I have always admired Helmut and Gisela's willingness to risk merging their personal lives and their academic lives for the benefit of students.

Looking back, I think the most important thing I learned from Helmut—in class, through his publications, and in subsequent trips to Greece, Turkey and Italy—is that scholars of Christian origins should not limit their study of Greco-Roman cities to "the holy land," "the cities of Paul" or "the seven churches of Asia." In other words, Priene is not less important than Ephesos simply because we have no record of Paul visiting that city. Because recent methodological trends have put considerable pressure on connecting the interpretations of biblical texts to narrow historical reconstructions, Helmut's emphasis on a more general—while at the same time more careful—knowledge of the urban context of nascent Christianity continues to stand up very well. Moreover, because of his rejection of "Paul-slept-here" approaches to archaeology—and his enormous energy—Helmut has forged relationships between field archaeologists and Christian origins scholars in the Aegean basin that have yielded unprecedented opportunities for students and important research for the discipline.

From my perspective, Helmut navigated an important transition in biblical studies. Obviously, his education at Marburg was firmly grounded in the History of Religions School. This education provided him—a student with unusual ability—with an intimidating knowledge of classical studies, biblical studies, and theology. During his career scholars of Christian origins came under increasing criticism for what Samuel Sandmel in his 1961 SBL Presidential Address famously called "parallelomania." However, instead of retreating from the study of the Greco-Roman context of Christian origins, it seems to me that Helmut worked assiduously to reduce the pressure his students felt to make direct parallels between texts and monuments—or other historical data. What mattered was not connecting the *bema* in Roman Corinth to the Acts account of Paul's appearance before Gallio, but to understanding how Roman governors and the *bema* functioned in Greek and Roman cities.

In the late eighties I was working on the Roman administration of non-Roman religions with Meyer Reinhold at Boston University and had decided to attempt a reading of Paul's letter to the Romans in light of this work for my dissertation. I recall a conversation with Helmut in which he asked me about the project—I think it was during a gathering of students from the 1987 seminar at their place in Lexington the following year. After listening to my description he simply encouraged me not "to claim too much." It was sage advice from a scholar who mediated the contributions of the History of Religions School to the next generation. I may not have followed his advice very well, but I never written an essay or given a presentation since without thinking of it.

One more characteristic of Helmut as a teacher stands out: rhetorically and intellectually, he is a formidable adversary. I recall winning only once. In the summer of 1991 the International SBL meeting was in Rome. After the meeting, Helmut was interested in visiting some excavations and museums in Italy with former students. After the meeting Helmut, Phil Sellew, Mimi Bonz, Steve Friesen, and I set out in my rental car for Hadrian's villa at Tivoli and the Bay of Naples. It was one of the best trips I have ever taken. After visiting the Naples museum we were looking for a place to stay where we could station ourselves for a few days while visiting Pompeii and Herculaneum. I took an exit off of the Autostrada in Naples that was taking us rather steeply above Naples. When my route decision was initially challenged by Helmut (who was sitting next to me), I said that I wanted to get us out of the city where we would be free of the congestion and smog of Naples—and maybe find a place with a view of the bay. Though this appealed to him, it quieted his objection for only a few miles. When he could stand it no longer, Helmut said: "There will be no places to stay up here; we must turn around!" I held nervously to my course. After a few more minutes, Helmut repeated more forcefully, "There will be no place up here!" I held course, but with an eye out for a place to turn around. Then, around the next switchback, a place appeared on the left and I pulled in. We found inexpensive lodging there with a terrific view of the Bay of Naples. And, each morning when we left for the day's activities the owner would report what he was planning to prepare for us to eat when we returned that evening—fresh rabbit on the first evening as I recall. We sat up late each night drinking wine, reflecting on what we had seen that day and listening to Helmut tell stories of the war, Marburg and Mr. and Mrs. Bultmann. On several occasions since that trip Helmut has retold that story, recounting his pessimism that we would find a place to stay up that road above Naples. Each time he ended the story by noting that my instincts turned out to be right. One reason for the success of Helmut's students, I think, is that they learned early on what it was like to come up against a formidable adversary, both in the classroom and afterward.

As I conclude, I should admit some trepidation in writing an essay of tribute for Helmut. A couple of years ago, after I delivered a paper at AAR/SBL, Helmut paid me a memorable compliment. He said that it was a good paper and that he learned something. True to my Southern roots I replied that it was very kind of him to say so and that I appreciated his gesture. Helmut immediately bristled and said, "I am not an American; I do not offer compliments to be kind!" Then, he turned abruptly and walked away. I wilted, fearing that I had blown one more opportunity to gain his respect. I know that Helmut has no time or patience for sappy tributes. Therefore, let me be clear: Helmut, I have learned much from you, and, although I am an American, this essay is not about being kind.

—*James Walters*

ALTHOUGH HELMUT Koester has educated an impressive roster of productive scholars, they differ so much from one another that one can't really speak of a "school of Helmut Koester." But I believe the honorand likes it that way. My strong love of archaeology and belief that its study can materially (as it were) improve the study of Christian origins nevertheless is an inheritance from my *Doktorvater*. His recommendation in 1991 to the former director of the Austrian Excavations at Ephesos, Gerhard Langmann, that I come to work with his team at the site, was a turning point in my studies. After a single season with Stefan Karwiese drawing walls and plans in the Church of Mary, I bit the bullet and learned to speak Turkish. This experience that Helmut generously provided for me, and his strong faith that I would succeed at it, have largely determined all my subsequent research. The dust got into my blood. Since then I have been able to publish a good range of archaeological artifacts illuminating the religions of Roman Asia Minor, and have developed excavation projects in and around Ephesos that have given each of my doctoral students the chance to participate in a dig. At the moment I am writing these lines from Ephesos.

Helmut's particular approach to archaeology represents a considerable contribution to New Testament studies. Before he began his work in this field, the focus of New Testament Archaeology was primarily on Galilee and Jerusalem in the lifetime of Jesus. As valuable as this knowledge is, Helmut was right to point out that the decisive spread and growth of early Christianity took place outside Palestine, in the cities and towns of Greece and Turkey. The cultural interaction that shaped early Christianity could better be understood by looking at contemporaneous religious life there. Second, Helmut's conviction was that one had to move beyond the mere use of archaeological artifacts as illustrations of the text. He taught his students to employ them in a reconstruction of the cultural, social and religious life of the Roman provinces that gave specific historical context to the early Christian message. This left a deep imprint on me as well. The drive to move beyond a text-dominated approach to the world of the New Testament has been an enduring leitmotif that has opened productive new perspectives in all my work.

An affinity for archaeology, however, is not a family trait that all Helmut's students share. When I reflect on him and on the years we spent together at Harvard, the quality that most comes to mind, and the one that I most wish to emulate, is his energy and dedication. Of course this was completely in evidence during the six weeks his classes spent touring Greece and Turkey. When I went on my first trip in 1987, I found out much to my dismay that I'd been sold a bill of goods with this course. I'd been given to believe that we'd spend mornings on site, relax at lunch, and retire in the afternoons to the beach. This was close to true, if one considers an appropriate lunch hour to be 2 or 3 in the afternoon, and a reasonable site visit to be six hours of lecturing by various foreign scholars standing out in the blazing sun. But instead of frolicking on the beach, we instead wanted after lunch to crawl into our hotel rooms to die. Death in the afternoon, indeed. There was, however, an unadvertised bonus educational component. After we finished eating lunch in this state of exhaustion, Helmut—and Gisela—would approach our tables to announce merrily that we'd not yet seen the acropolis. One of the unforgettable lessons of the trip was that every ancient city had an acropolis, which was predictably in a very high place. But I also learned that a healthy young Minnesotan, serious aficionado of cross-county skiing in subzero temperatures, could be left in the dust by these two "senior citizens." Step for step, I just could not keep up with them.

In fact, the pace of this particular trip was so widely recognized by the students as an aberrance that Kimberley Patton christened it the "No Relax Tour," from an aphorism intoned to her by a Greek guard during a site visit, as she lay down to rest on a low wall at an ancient monastery: "No relax!" he shouted. That summed up the general experience, and years later, some members of that 1987 trip still share a suite together at the SBL national meeting in the eponymously named "No Relax Suite," as a sort of extended longitudinal group therapy. Nevertheless, these journeys were extraordinarily popular with students, despite the breakneck pace, because Helmut has a charming way of making his pursuits seem attractive to others. How else could one explain the appeal of visiting a new site every other day and staying in hotels with a sometimes less than optimal commitment to toilet paper and hot water?

What was Helmut's secret? When I came to Harvard, I remember being surprised initially at how open and generous Helmut was to his students. It was common knowledge that the key to his office, L-12, hung behind the desk at Andover Harvard library, in my time perversely attached to a pink plastic palm tree, and could be requested (I confess I used it to browse his pretty comprehensive set of the *ANRW*). I also must have been to his house more than a dozen times during my six years of graduate study and three years at the Society of Fellows: evenings of music, dinners with students, Easter egg hunts. At one memorable Thanksgiving I sat at a huge long table filled with international scholars, famous first-rate academics, who'd come there after the SBL meeting, at which, courtesy of Edward Hobbs, I drank wines most of which were about my age. Helmut and Gisela had a gift for forming a community around themselves, and using their home to continue their life at the university. The company of their scholar friends was in itself educational.

In retrospect I see that Helmut's openness taught me lessons as valuable as any in the seminar room. I was able to observe the manner in which a scholarly life could be lived, and how scholarship could be integrated with other aspects of one's personality and interests. This is what Max Weber aptly described in his essay, "Wissenschaft als Beruf," "Scholarship as a Way of Life." Only later, well into my career, have I realized how uncommon Helmut is among academics. I know far more about his work habits, and his goals and commitments, than I do about those of any of my present colleagues. We students knew not to call before 8 or 8:30, because normal working hours for Helmut ran well into the night. He once told me emphatically, "All of the most important work I do for the future of our department happens between midnight and 2 a.m.!" He also emphasized that one must have one's library at home in order to be productive.

Over the years, I observed that scholarly productivity was just one facet of Helmut's generally energetic demeanor. He was active in so many ways: deeply informed about international politics, seriously knowledgeable about classical music, committed to the work of Amnesty

International, engaged in community work and preaching at University Lutheran. He was not idle in manual labor, either. Given my own Midwestern background, I actually understood his accounts of the impressive annual yield of his vegetable garden, measured in kilos. I called him up one day when he must have been close to seventy, and to my surprise and amusement, had to wait while Gisela fetched him from chopping wood out back, with an ax!

When Helmut retired, I was certain that he'd never leave the classroom, but even I did not expect him to participate in four—or is it five—"last" trips to Greece with the research team. I learned from Helmut that scholarly productivity results from an active engagement with the rest of one's life, and with one's community, especially one's students. It was clear to me that Helmut's research is not a sterile or isolated pursuit, and that his teaching is integrally related to the rest of his life. For him, teaching and research are significant, interesting, and fun. The family trait I wish most to inherit from my *Doktorvater* is the ability, the consciousness, to find scholarship energizing in and of itself, year after year. If I can emulate this, I will have become a true student of my teacher.

Happy birthday, Helmut. I hope to be able to write for you again on your ninetieth.

—*Chris Thomas*

Jennifer K. Berenson Maclean

AFTER BEING accepted to the program in New Testament and Christian Origins at Harvard in the spring of 1988, I happened to be traveling to Boston as part of my job as an editor for a scientific publisher. I hoped to be able to meet some of my future professors—especially Helmut—whose work had drawn me to study at Harvard. I cannot remember precisely how it was all arranged, but despite the fact that it was Gisela's birthday (apologies to you, Gisela, many years late), Helmut wanted to drive in from Lexington to meet me. I was flattered and, not surprisingly, quite nervous. As an undergraduate I had heard horror stories of professors moving, retiring, or even dying and leaving their graduate students in the lurch. And it was obvious from Helmut's publication record and stature in the field that he could be ready for retirement. I had asked him on the phone some weeks before the trip, having carefully chosen my phrasing, "How long do you plan on remaining active in the department?" (read: are you planning on retiring soon or are you terminally ill?). Helmut had assured me that he would see me through my dissertation, but what else would a senior professor say to a prospective graduate student? I made my way over to Andover Hall a bit early and sat outside on a bench as I waited for Helmut to arrive. After a few minutes, a bent, gray-haired, old man emerged from the parking lot, shuffled toward the library, and went up the steps and in toward Helmut's office. My heart sank. Eventually I screwed up my courage to introduce myself to Helmut. Imagine my surprise when I knocked on the door and was greeted by a completely different man. Despite his years (he was in his early sixties), Helmut was neither bent nor tired, but the energetic and enthusiastic man I knew all through graduate school.

This enthusiasm spilled out from Helmut regularly, whether in seminar, in discussions at his office, or on the archaeological trip to Greece and Turkey. I had already been to Greece prior to my turn on "the trip" in 1989. My previous visit to Corinth had been memorable, meeting the potter who imitates Exekias and other ancient masters and ordering the most delicious yogurt with honey at a nearby taverna. At the time I had not considered hiking to the top of Acrocorinth, even though I did spend a good deal of time among the Roman period ruins. But on the trip with Helmut, his energy level, which was formidable, dictated the effort required by his students. Out the door early in the morning, he let us stop for lunch only at 3:00 or sometimes even 4:00 p.m. so as not to miss any chance to visit the archaeological sites. And at Corinth, even after a long day on site, it was clear that we were going up to Acrocorinth—despite what we learned were its meager remains and despite the fact he had done it many times before. Chain-smoking all the way to the top, Helmut—I remember the image of a mountain goat came to mind—outpaced most of us, including me and my aching knees. It was becoming clear that the enthusiasm and energy he put into his own work would be expected of us as well.

This, it seems, was Helmut's method of inspiring his students. I cannot think of a time or remember hearing of a time when Helmut chewed out a student for inferior work or inadequate effort; you could expect criticism for your work—and biting criticism at that—but not verbal flagellation for poor effort or less than appropriate dedication. Instead Helmut's own enthusiasm, energy, and dedication to the field functioned like a Bultmannian moment of *krisis*, confronting graduate students and forcing upon them a decision of whether or not to try to live up to Helmut's high expectations. I cannot say whether other students felt this way, but I know this reflects the effect Helmut's demeanor had upon me. Enthusiasm for biblical studies in the context of the ancient world and high expectations for students are both a part of my own teaching, although interaction with undergraduates at my own institution requires a bit more cajoling of students than was ever evident at HDS. Perhaps my pedagogy is modeled less on the Johannine Jesus and more on a Synoptic Jesus?

Although academics laud the value of openness to new ideas, at times that openness is in word only. The bold breakthroughs of the past slowly become the unquestioned dogma of today. I now believe it is idealistic and even inappropriate to expect a scholar to maintain openness in all arenas at all times, so I am not criticizing Helmut when I say that at his best he modeled for his students the kind of scholarly openness upon which academia is founded. For me this became most clear as I struggled through the dissertation. Although it was not the most logical topic to pursue with Helmut, whose primary interests lay in other areas of the early Christian literature, I wrote my dissertation on the post-Pauline tradition. We met regularly in his office to discuss my work; I sat on the "hot seat" (it literally bore that label), and the two of us engaged in heated discussion for the hour. By the end of the process I was thrilled to hear Helmut acknowledge that what he feared was a fruitless mode of analysis had yielded important and interesting results. The point here is not the vindication of my dissertation, but the demonstration that true scholarship entails openness and the willingness to be persuaded. I hope that I still model that same attitude for my students when I approach the final years of my career.

—Jennifer Maclean

*K*LAROS, *M*AY *1991*: It is a warm morning in early summer as the Harvard New Testament archaeological seminar sets out from Kusadasi, Turkey where we have been staying in order to visit Ephesus under the direction of Helmut Koester. These have been full and complex days—my first visit to Turkey, bringing to life an ancient city that I had known only on paper, through slides, and from maps and published inscriptions, but also involving visits to carpet showrooms, the tastes of Turkish food, and the warm waters of the Aegean. Now the seminar has piled into two vans to head north along the coast toward modern Bergama and the riches of Pergamum. Helmut has suggested that first we take a short detour to Klaros, a site just a short distance from Ephesus and one that he professes that he has never visited. As we drive, he asks me to read aloud the pages on Klaros from our "bible": Ekrem Akurgal's *Ancient Civilizations and the Ruins of Turkey*. This short description, however, hardly prepares us for what we find: the oracular temples of Apollo and Artemis half underwater from the recent rains, fragments of the monumental statues—a sandal-clad foot of the god, the goddess's well-draped torso—and the texts of second-century oracular queries and responses inscribed upon columns. Only later do I take in the importance of the site, its vital role in the life of the cities of Asia Minor in the imperial period, and indeed its "voice" in responding to the plagues of the later second century. On that morning, it is an experience of sheer exploration and discovery, without an expert or a prepared paper, but simply the pleasure of pointing out details to one another, testing ideas *in situ*, and building on all that we have learned in the previous days and months.

I begin this short piece in tribute to Helmut Koester with this oracular vignette because it encapsulates what is in my mind one of the most important aspects of his teaching and research, namely, his willingness to delve into unexplored territory and to teach others by leading them through the process of discovery. To borrow a metaphor from the Letter to the Hebrews, he is an *archēgos*, leading others into greater knowledge and experience by gathering them up in his train. There is, of course, much "material" that I learned from Helmut, including much about the religions, cultures, and political workings of the Hellenistic and Roman worlds that was made tangible and visible through the archaeological seminar. But as I reflect on how my teaching and scholarship have been shaped by working with Helmut, it is particularly this model of drawing others into a new adventure that stands at the center. At the root, I experienced it as a mode of education grounded in trust, wherein he expressed a certain assurance that we were sure to discover something worthwhile simply by the process of disciplined inquiry and reflection. As on that day at Klaros, he also demonstrated for his students this bold spirit of exploration in his articles, his lectures, and the discussions he initiated in seminars. I recall with warmth his repeated exhortation to me to be courageous, not least in putting ideas and observations together in new ways. It was also an encouragement to boldness in returning again and again to the primary texts, leaving to one side for the moment the morass of secondary literature, in order to read afresh. Coming one afternoon to his office overwhelmed by all that had been written on 1 Corinthians and the Lord's Supper, I was surprised and heartened to hear Helmut say, "Don't worry about all that; you don't need all that. You'll figure out what of the literature you need once you know what you want to say about the text." This trust—both in the process of critical inquiry and in the infinite resources that the text or artifact has yet to reveal—gives me great hope for the future of such a intensely worked-over field of study as the field of New Testament and Early Christianity. I am deeply gratefully to Helmut for giving me this orientation toward scholarship and in my teaching.

Oracles themselves are the second reason why I began this reflection with the snapshot from Klaros. In the study of ancient oracular utterances a number of areas of inquiry come together: genre, religious speech, the establishment of authority, the cultivation of civic identity, divine revelation, to name a few. Although Helmut and I never worked together explicitly on a study of oracles in the ancient world, they serve as a focal point for the key areas of inquiry that he nurtured in my scholarship. A directed reading course one year on the precursors of form criticism—among them Heitmüller, Herder, and Eichhorn—helped me to connect the study of marked speech as religious practice with some of the persistent questions of New Testament scholarship set in motion by Dibelius and Bultmann. Attention to the performative character of an enigmatic utterance gave me particular appreciation for the traditions of Jesus' sayings, thus coupling other aspects of my education in folklore and classics with some of Helmut's earliest work on the transmission of Jesus' sayings. He also taught me a special concern for the interrelation between revelatory utterance, authority, civic identity, and canon—a nexus of issues that informed the approach that Jennifer Berenson Maclean and I took to understanding Philostratus's *Heroikos*, a text to which Helmut introduced us. The interchange of ideas around these topics as I shaped my dissertation—I remember in particular some rich discussions over lunch with Gregory Nagy and Helmut—not only guided my own approach to passion traditions in earliest Christianity but also sparked fresh ideas for Helmut's own work on the very beginnings of Christian community. The "oracle" thus epitomizes for me some of the intellectual approaches most important to my understanding of early Christianity, shaped and honed under Helmut's direction and encouragement.

"Describe, describe, describe," these were Helmut's instructions to us as we studied archaeological remains. Similarly they were his instructions whenever we were tempted to jump too quickly to a conclusion about a text. Such was also his approach, I learned, whenever he taught in less academic settings, for example, with groups of clergy and lay people in the preaching and exegesis workshops held over the years at the Foundation for Biblical Research in Charlestown, New Hampshire. As he invited me to participate in teaching these bimonthly seminars, I came to know another side of Helmut—his passion for making biblical studies accessible to preachers and Christian educators, along with his commitment to supporting the life of congregations. It became apparent to me, moreover, that when he taught in these workshops he expected the same rigor of inquiry and exploration that he did in a graduate seminar, grounded firmly in the process of careful description and the testing of hypotheses against what one saw. Helmut's dedication to this kind of teaching and his witness in offering the very best of biblical scholarship to strengthen the day-to-day life of communities of faith has over the years given me courage to do the same. As a scholarly *archēgos* not only has he set an example for such work, indeed for the entire endeavor of scholarship, but he has also opened a way and enabled many others to enter with understanding into the wonders of the early Christian world.

—*Ellen Aitken*

SHELLY MATTHEWS

G*NOMAI DIAPHOROI—KAI GE* . . . A quick review of lessons learned from Helmut Koester: Rocks are texts; the Red Hall at Pergamon, the Isis aretalogies, the Priene inscription celebrating the birth of Augustus are all part of the social complex in which Christianity was constructed; the twenty-seven books of the New Testament, standing alone, are a very thin guide to the history of early Christianity; lines drawn between apocryphal and canonical literature have no heuristic value; the readings of the early fathers and the so-called heretics are important and precious clues for interpreting the earliest Jesus material; assessing the roles and agency of women in the ancient world is a crucial scholarly enterprise (and here I add that Helmut always supported his many women doctoral students, and always encouraged and supported whatever interest they might have in the intersection of women's studies and the study of early Christianity); New Testament theology must remain a vital discipline, in view of the importance of this book to faith communities, and especially in view of its prophetic potential to speak truth to power; but at the same time the scholar of early Christianity can never be beholden to a particular faith community's theological assertions as a framework for analysis.

In attempting to sort through all of these lessons and bind them under one guiding metaphor, I find myself drawn to Helmut's classic and programmatic essay, "GNOMAI DIAPHOROI." It has now been forty years since its initial publication (*HTR* [1965]). Yet, in spite of research developments in the field, the essay still serves as an invaluable guide to the regional, doctrinal, and literary diversity of early Christianity. But more than the particulars of the essay, the principle undergirding it—that there were "different opinions," a multitude of diverse voices involved in creative reflection, deliberation, debate, contest, struggle—both shapes my approach to the ancient sources, and allows me to believe that scholars of ancient Christianity have something of immediate relevance to contribute to our contemporary, polyglot, post-modern age. As Helmut underscored, early Christianity's chosen self-description was *ekklēsia*, a term evoking the deliberating body of citizens of the Greek polis.

114

In my own scholarship, the principle of GNOMAI DIAPHOROI prompts, on the one hand, work to resurrect the voices of some of those early debaters whose perspectives ultimately came to be obliterated from the canonical historical record. On the other, it prompts work to dislodge hegemonic voices of canonical scripture, to situate them among many different opinions, so that they are not granted authorization as sole witnesses, whose version of events must be accepted as the one that is natural and obvious.

Dislodging the canonical version of events is a key concern of my current work on the book of Acts. For instance, I set Acts' version of how the mission to the Gentiles is inaugurated next to the related, and considerably later, aetiology of the Gentile mission in the Pseudo-Clementine *Recognitions* 1.27–71, in order to underscore that Acts is arguing for a particular version of Christianity, not reflecting a Christian consensus. While the *Recognitions* 1.27–71 is dependent upon Acts, this author steals and rearranges bricks from the Christianity constructed in Acts for a different sort of construction project. Of special interest is the way that *R* 1.27–71 tones down Acts' hostility toward non-believing Jews. It is not too strong to say that, with few exceptions, Acts depicts non-believing Jews as morally depraved barbarians prone to stasis, and stiff-necked prophet persecutors excluded from salvation. *R* 1.27–71 clearly holds a different opinion. Unlike the history of Israel recounted by Stephen in Acts 7, *R* 1.27–71's historiographic recitation does not depict the people as congenitally disobedient and idolatrous, and the prophet persecution motif is entirely dropped; differently from Acts, *R* 1.27–71 does not devalue Torah observance; the accusations leveled by Peter in Acts against all Israel as Christ killers are replaced by assertions that culpability for the crucifixion is borne by a more limited group (*R* 1.41.2).

Moreover, *R* 1.27–71 indicates at least some resistance to Acts' exclusivist views on salvation. For instance, *R* 1.52.1–3 concerns the status of the righteous who lived before Christ's appearance, and reassures, in a manner not unlike Justin Martyr, that Christ has always been with the righteous, even before his advent. More remarkable is the expression of relative tolerance toward those Jews in the text who do not accept Jesus' messianic status. In a debate staged in the temple between Jews who believe in Jesus and Jews who do not, the Jesus-believing Barabbas is depicted as follows:

> Barabbas . . . exhorted the people not to hate and dishonor Jesus, 'For it is better for the one who does not know Jesus to be the Christ not to hate him, since God has appointed a reward for love and not hate. Further, since he took a body from the Jews and became a Jew, the destruction that God will bring on the one who hates him will not be a small one. (*Rec.* 1.60.5–7 [trans. F. Stanley Jones (1995), 95])

Notice that the view stated here, differently from Acts, is not that "all who refuse to *believe* in Jesus are condemned," but rather all who *hate* Jesus. Instead of spewing vitriol at all Jews who refuse to grant messianic status to Jesus, Barabbas acknowledges those holding that position while still pleading for some common ground between this group and his own—if you cannot accept our version of truth, at least refrain from hating Jesus.

In analyzing the changes that *R* 1.27–71 effects upon Acts with respect to Jewish/Christian identity questions, it seems safe to say that the later text regards the rhetoric of the earlier as unnecessarily extreme. Though this text still acknowledges a border between Jesus believers and non-believing Jews, it prefers one without the injurious barbed wire spilling over the top, one low enough that it can be talked across. Privileging a text such as this in reconstructing varieties of Christianity makes it possible to argue that, in spite of what Acts suggests, relations between believing and non-believing Jews could sometimes be irenic and that Jewish-Christianity did not flower only to die off quickly in the first century.

This, of course, makes our picture of early Christianity more richly variegated. It also serves as a useful point of departure for contemporary interfaith conversations among Jews and Christians. I offer this very brief and cursory comparison of two documents with competing views concerning Judaeo-Christianity as one instance of a path one might follow, should one adopt the dual premise that in the study of early Christianity canonical sources do not receive special privilege and that the movement was marked by diversification from the start. Professor Koester offered his programmatic essay as "blue print for further work in the history of early Christian theology" ("GNOMAI DIAPHOROI," 199). These blueprints are still guiding early Christian scholarship into the twenty-first century.

I close with an anecdote set in a locale that should strike resonant chords with most of Professor Koester's students—a restaurant in Selçuk after a long day spent at the excavated sites of Ephesos, May of 1991. The engagement with the magnificent ruins of this city prompted the following hypothetical question during dinner: if we were given the opportunity to recover one, and only one, text of ancient Christianity that is no longer extant, which one would you choose? Helmut did not hesitate: "Q." Neither did I: "The report from Chloe's people." These differing choices, perhaps, reflect something of our divergent scholarly interests and perspectives; but of course, if given the opportunity, he would gladly hear from Chloe as well. In gratitude and admiration I pay tribute to Helmut as a scholar who has devoted considerable care and energy to the task of enabling a multitude of "different opinions" to be given voice.

—*Shelly Matthews*

IT IS my extreme pleasure to have this opportunity to offer a few reflections of my experiences with Professor Helmut Koester during my
studies at HDS from 1986–1997 in celebration of his 80th birthday. If
I might propose a particular theme appropriate for my experiences with
this renowned scholar, it would perhaps be the biblical theme of "promise
and fulfillment" or perhaps a less theologically laden but no less appropriate theme of "commitment and actualization." The reasons for such a
theme and assessment of my experiences with Helmut Koester will perhaps become evident in the course of my reflections.

I matriculated at HDS in the fall of 1986 after completing a B.A.
in comparative religion at the University of Wisconsin-Milwaukee, in-
tending to complete the Master of Theological Studies (M.T.S.) degree
and return home to Milwaukee, Wisconsin and begin pastoral ministry.
While I had nurtured an intense interest in the New Testament during my undergraduate studies, which was cultivated further after taking
Helmut's course "Religious Thought in the Ancient Christian Period" in
the fall of 1986, I did not have aspirations to pursue doctoral studies in
this area. As a matter of fact, I was not quite sure what I was going to do
academically once I completed the M.T.S. degree. This is where the commitment and guidance of Helmut comes in to play. In the last semester
of the two-year M.T.S. program (spring 1988) I came to Helmut's office
and informed him that I was interested in pursuing a doctorate in New
Testament. While my academic record was adequate but not outstand-
ing, Helmut informed me that my problem was not academics but a
matter of poor course selection during my M.T.S. studies; namely, I had
not taken many courses with HDS professors who would be informed
about and could vouch for my work, and perhaps might even sit on the
Committee for the Study of Religion. My previous lack of direction and
proper preparation posed a challenge to my newly conceived goals for
doctoral studies. However all was not lost.

In his office on that important day (at least for me!), Helmut proposed a plan for me to actualize my goals. First, he gently chided me for
not enrolling in the Master of Divinity (M.Div.) program, knowing that

I was already a licensed minister in the National Baptist denomination. I had operated at that time under the naïve assumption that since my denomination did not require the M.Div. degree for ordination, I did not necessarily need the credentialing that the M.Div. degree conferred. Helmut informed me otherwise, suggesting that such a degree is a professional degree that would be beneficial to me in the long run regardless of my own denominational requirements. In addition, it would also allow me to take some of the courses needed to strengthen my application to the doctoral program in New Testament. I followed his advice and after receiving the M.T.S. in 1988, I enrolled in the M.Div. program in the spring of 1989. As I have reflected over the years about the advice he provided me that day, especially about pursuing the M.Div. degree and the access and opportunities for ministry I have gained on account of it, I remain indebted to him to this day for his insight. I also sensed that a subtle commitment was fostered that day to see me through the process of preparing for doctoral studies in New Testament.

I now had a new opportunity to prepare for my newly conceived and acknowledged goals. Helmut assisted me in planning a schedule of courses designed to make up for deficiencies in my studies and to work with other HDS professors who could become more familiar with my work. I remember clearly what he told me at the start of the M.Div. program: "Take these courses and get A's." Fortunately I did what was requested! After three semesters of intense but fruitful study, I was awarded the M.Div. degree in the spring of 1990, and was accepted into the doctoral program at HDS scheduled to start in the fall of the same year. This was the first experience of commitment and actualization. Two other examples follow.

In the spring of 1991 (immediately after the first Gulf War), several of Helmut's graduate students, including myself, were afforded the opportunity to spend six weeks in Greece and Turkey. To be sure, Helmut's excursions to Greece are almost legendary. I recall fondly that on one evening while having dinner, Helmut stated that those New Testament doctoral students present would perhaps be his last advisees before his semi-retirement. Most notable to me was his comment that he wanted not only to guide us through the completion of the program but also to see that we find employment. This he did for me one year after I completed qualifying exams and the submission and acceptance of my dissertation prospectus. Having just begun the dissertation in fall of 1995, I was stopped by Helmut in front of Divinity Hall at the end of the fall Convocation ; he asked me had I heard from Tulane University yet? I was a bit taken aback because I had not been in contact with any university nor had I been on the job market. I asked him why I would be hearing from them. My surprised look initiated a smile from him, and he then stated that I would be hearing from them soon because he had recommended me for a teaching position. There was a mixture of excitement and anxiety because I was in the initial stages of the writing process. This anxiety, I later discovered, was not unfounded. In December of 1995 I was interviewed and was offered a tenure-track position at Tulane University, contingent upon completing the dissertation in the first year. I was now employed. Even then I recalled Helmut's commitment to find employment for his students. This was the second experience of commitment and actualization.

The final example unfolded near the end of my first year of teaching at Tulane (spring 1997) and writing the dissertation. As many ABD's can affirm, this is quite a daunting task and I was pushing time to the limit, however not by choice. In late April 1997 I called Helmut and informed him that I had finally completed the penultimate draft of the dissertation and was ready to submit it for review. In a measured tone he informed me that there was not enough time for the committee to read and schedule a dissertation defense before his biennial trip to Greece, which was scheduled in just about a week or so. The news was devastating, especially in view of the fact that my continued employment depended upon a successful thesis defense before the end of the semester. I was at a loss. But then I remembered Helmut's commitment to see that I was employed. Perhaps his commitment could be extended to see that I remained employed. I called him back and stated such in our conversation. He told me to email the dissertation. He called about two days later and told me to get on a plane at my earliest convenience to defend my thesis. He had come through again! I passed the thesis defense and was able to keep my job and enjoy many fruitful years of teaching and writing at Tulane. (Ten years to be exact: 1996–2006, before the Katrina hurricane altered my plans and the plans of many!) For this and other experiences I owe him a debt of gratitude.

So it is with great appreciation that I offer these reflections in honor of Professor Helmut Koester on his 80th birthday. While this account does not include the many dinners at his home that I shared with several of his other advisees, or the many memories of the New Testament Doctoral Seminar, or especially the archaeological tour to Greece and Turkey, it does offer a glimpse of his commitment to students endeavoring to join the guild of New Testament scholars.

With your commitment and guidance I was able to actualize my goals. Thanks, Helmut, and congratulations as you receive this volume as a well-deserved honor.

—Demetrius Williams

I F YOU end up spending any time at all with Helmut Koester, *prepare to be changed.* . . .

With his ground-breaking, two-volume *Introduction to the New Testament* translated and then retranslated into several languages as just one example, it goes without saying that this professor has significantly changed the intellectual landscape of New Testament studies. I could easily expound upon the contributions of Helmut's scholarship or explain how Helmut's lectures influenced the academic thinking of his many students, but I wish to explore, instead, the innumerable ways in which Helmut's presence can change someone personally as well.

Change is especially inevitable if a student is lucky enough to participate in one of Helmut's infamous expeditions to ancient archaeological sites in Greece and Turkey. Before the class ever actually encounters the specific sites themselves, Helmut has already motivated students to do their own kind of digging . . . in the libraries at Harvard. With the dust of a thousand books still on your hands, he then whets your appetite by taking you to site after site with his own slides from previous visits, until you can see yourself walking the Arcadian way in your mind's eye before you have ever set foot in that country. If you spend time with Helmut, prepare to be inspired.

In fact, it was because of Helmut that I became a doctoral student in the first place. His encouragement for me to do archaeological research for him (and in the process actually receive pay for doing what I enjoyed) required that I enter a program rather than just take classes. This, however, was not a surprising development for me since, originally, it was archaeology that drew me more intensely in biblical studies. Years before meeting Helmut, I received a flyer in the mail and became intrigued by a course entitled "Archaeology of the Holy Land." In that class I experienced one of those life-changing and defining moments, as the professor passed around artifacts and captured my imagination. The collection of exhibits included the usual shards, lamps, and small jars, but most amazing was a beautiful clay object, the size of a large thumb, shaped like a barbell, but with a pea rolling around inside of it. He asked us what we imagined it could be, and, when no one even ventured a guess, he explained it was a baby's rattle from the time of Abraham and Sarah. From that point on I was hooked.

It was ten years and an MTS degree later when I met Helmut for the first time. I had returned to the Boston area and considered pursuing advanced studies, which, of course, included his biblical archaeology course. The experience proved to be a profound one. Helmut makes the world his classroom and thereby brings depth to what he teaches. Helmut and archaeology are a potent mix for beginning scholars, not to be drunk lightly. If you are around him for very long, prepare to be challenged, not only mentally, but also physically and otherwise.

The Helmut archaeological expeditions were indeed a challenge in every sense of the word. You carried by hand whatever you brought on the trip. Those who were wise brought only a couple of shirts and a pair of pants. Some of the rest of us dragged around all our baggage, ultimately learning a painful lesson since Helmut rarely spent more than a night or two in one spot. The trip was all planes and trains and automobiles when it was not on foot. Helmut knew everybody along the way and he knew the cheapest places to stay. By the end of the day, when we had thoroughly traversed yet another archaeological site and were sitting exhausted and ready to crawl back to the hotel with the ubiquitous cold showers, you could inevitably hear Helmut say something like, "Oh wait, we haven't climbed up to the top of the acropolis yet . . . who wants to go?" Like the Energizer bunny, he just keeps going and going, pulling more out of you than you ever knew you had. Those small excursions allowed us the opportunity to view famous works of art located in high and out of the way places, such as the Hosios David in Thessaloniki.

My favorite parts of the trip were in the evenings, when we could relax, sit beneath the stars and sheltering grape vines, and discuss papers or events while partaking of retsina and Greek bread dipped in tzatziki. We could laugh about how we had quizzically looked at each other whenever our guide repeatedly referred to this important "centimeter," until it eventually dawned on us that he was referring to "St. Demeter." These times balanced the frantic pace of the trip, which nervous tension exacerbated further until you finally made your on-site presentation. Once you had finished, the rest of the trip became much more enjoyable. Even then, Helmut did not let you rest on your laurels, but continued to challenge you, expand your horizons, and inspire you beyond your own boundaries. If you hang around Helmut long enough, you will have experiences you will not soon forget. He not only teaches you, but also allows you to teach yourself and introduces you to others from whom you can learn.

In addition to exposure to the accumulation of Helmut's academic experience, students also benefit from the scores of social relationships that he has built up over the decades, whether it be religious leaders, archaeologists, museum curators, or a multitude of restaurant owners in small Greek and Turkish villages who remember him and welcome his group with open arms. Because of Helmut's contacts, for example, we were able to rub elbows with some of the world's best archaeologists. At Philippi, he introduced us to Professor Bakirtzis, from whom we learned the lesson of observation before deduction: "Never begin with your interpretation, just describe . . . describe . . . describe." This experience reinforced for us the importance of attention to detail in an entirely new way. Sometimes we were even able to interact with the archaeologist who had actually excavated the site we were visiting, which is what happened in my case. I will never forget the night before I was to make my presentation when Helmut returned from a preliminary visit to Pergamon to tell me with a smile, "Guess who I have arranged to respond to your presentation personally . . . Wolfgang Radt himself." My heart leapt to my throat and I grew pale, knowing that he might be much more invested in defending his own interpretation of the site than hearing my alternative explanation. As it turned out, he was very open. It was a great experience I hope never to repeat. As usual, that night we talked about it over food and drink.

Helmut knows the spirit of hospitality. Not only is he always building warm friendships throughout the archaeological world, but he continues to do so at home as well. His was the first professor's home I ever visited at Harvard, as he and Gisela, with their incredible hospitality, frequently opened their doors to students. If you hang around Helmut for very long, you will meet Gisela, who helps him change the world one student at a time. They are a valuable pair of ambassadors for scholarship.

Helmut not only generously extends his hospitality, but he also willingly shares his time, such that if you are around Helmut for very long, prepare to be mentored. In addition to mentoring you during class and on expeditions, he puts in overtime as well. Some of my favorite moments include sessions at the Chinese restaurant on Massachusetts Avenue discussing portions of my dissertation, hearing challenging questions, and subsequently seeing things in a new way.

So, in the same way the baby rattle made the biblical narratives real in a new, much more concrete way, so, too, did my time with Helmut in an exponential way. The archaeological experiences, the hours of research, and the culminating food and discussions not only made biblical studies more tangible, but more intense and alive. These transformations are due, in large part, to how full of life Helmut is and how much he loves what he does. His enthusiasm will change, inspire, challenge, and mentor you. It has done so for generations of students.

When you spend time with Helmut, prepare never to be the same.

—Ann Graham Brock

W ALKING THE *ancient city* . . .
As he understands Paul to have rejected the patron-client relations of the ancient Mediterranean world, Helmut Koester too has tried
to reject a patronage system, rife with injustice and economic inequality,
that is everywhere evident in the world he studies. Usually over a lovely
Chinese dinner, or perhaps at the home that he and Gisela frequently,
generously open to all, serving treats from their garden, one hears: "My
students are not my clients, but my friends."

In that spirit of friendship, understood in modern, democratic terms,
Koester took many of us to Greece and Turkey—many of us who now
do the same for our students. Alongside his good friend Charalambos
Bakirtzis, he insisted that members of the seminar *observe*. Hot and tired,
standing in the dry sun with the delicious Mediterranean just visible
from the corner of the eye, generations of students would pause before
what looked like a hopeless ruin. Don't walk over a crumbling wall when
you can find the doorway. Don't build an edifice before you have carefully taken into account the fragments that remain. Hypothesize what
is lost; engage the imagination. Students who moments ago wanted to
tromp away over the humble, weedy yellow chamomile instead stay to
exegete the ruins. Which way did a door open? Were aisles blocked with
barricades that restricted sight? Where might the cult statue or altar of
a temple have been? We consider what it feels like to be a human body
before such an altar, standing behind a barrier, traversing such a building, approaching a statue, walking the ancient city (see Vitruvius, *De
architectura* 4.5.1).

The archaeology of the early Christian world does not start with
the catacombs of Rome or with a single earliest Christian structure. The
archaeology of the New Testament or early Christian world starts with
consideration of how those who first thought that Jesus was the *Christos*
lived and moved and had their being as they wove their way between
the cities of the Roman Empire. Koester's insistence on Roman-period
archaeological remains, on the one hand, and his rejection of the patronage system of the ancient world, on the other, encourage us toward new

ways of reading early Christian literature within the built environment
of cities under Rome. Such a reading would not allow us to be seduced
quickly by the beauty of the cool marble statuary or the massiveness of
the imperial cult temples, built high on platforms like the Pergamene
Trajaneum or the Ephesian Temple to the Flavian Sebastoi, impressing
the city and impressing themselves upon the city. Metropolitan centers
under the Roman Empire bristled with new buildings, refurbished ones,
and statuary, an insensate, ghostly, often over life-sized "other popula-
tion." You could not walk the city without running into countless gods
and goddesses, emperors, elites, and emperors and elites in the guise of
gods and goddesses. But we would not align with the scopophilia of the
elite, who wish to see from the heights and who wish to *be seen*, especially
in statuary form, crowding the most prestigious urban spaces.

One example of the power and spectacle in the Roman world—not
necessarily one that many Christians saw, but one that contained many
of the discourses they engaged—is the Forum of Trajan. The Forum,
completed by Trajan's successor, Hadrian, included a monumental gate,
several porticoes surrounding a colossal equestrian statue of Trajan, the
Basilica Ulpia, a judicial court; behind that, the double library of Trajan
with a courtyard containing Trajan's column; further on was the Temple
of Trajan. This Forum had many functions (see James Packer's two-volume *Forum of Trajan in Rome*, 1997). Its unusual column celebrated
Roman triumphs over Dacia. On the basilica of justice, also an unusual
feature for an imperial forum, barbarian Dacians, bodies of pavonazzetto,
heads and hands of white marble, stood pathos-inspiring and humbly
captive. They were embedded architecturally between deified emperors
and stood under bronze military standards. Walking in the forum, one's
eyes would nearly have been pierced by all the weaponry on the basilica's
roof—the military trophies, as well as the quadriga and two bigae, a statue of Trajan, right arm raised in salute, likely above it all.

In this Forum Hadrian burned the official records of debts owed to
the state; Marcus destroyed tax records and adorned the Forum with statues, including one to his tutor Marcus Frontus. Here Commodus handed
out imperial donations and presided in the east apse or *atrium libertatis*
of the Basilica Ulpia. New laws were posted here and *summi viri* or pub-

lic heroes were honored with statues. Thus the Forum of Trajan was the chief judicial center, a religious center full of statuary which blurred the imperial family with the gods, a key site of knowledge/*paideia*, a place to recognize an emperor's philosophical teacher, and also a proclamation of triumph. In the heart of *the* city of the empire, we find a concatenation of rhetoric, materially expressed, of imperial power, justice, benefaction, piety—all under what we might see as signs of violence.

Instead of being seduced by elite messages such as these, drawn into their scopophilia, we would read our early Christian literature while walking the city, weaving our way through its centers but also its alleys, conscious that some human bodies were more vulnerable than others as they traversed the city. Justin's *First Apology* (ca. 150–155) begins with an affirmation and a challenge to the kind of claims made by Trajan's Forum. At the start he addresses Antoninus as *Eusebeia*, or Piety, and Marcus Aurelius as *Philosophia*, or philosophy, and makes reference to their love of the (conquered) Greek *paideia* or culture which was such a commodity at the time (*1 Apol.* 1.1). Later, Justin states his main point directly:

> We are not flattering you with these writings, nor are we joining in battle for its own sake, but we have come forward to speak, asking [you] to offer a judgment after a precise and exacting reckoning, seized neither by the desire to please people who hold on to superstitions, nor by irrational impulse and long-held, evil rumor, with the result that you cast a vote against your own selves. (2.3; my translation)

If they are misled by *deisidaimonia*, the "pious" emperors are not truly pious. They become uncultured—without *paideia* and philosophy—and superstitious, superstition being the equally problematic reverse of the atheism of which Christians are accused (Plutarch, *On Superstition*). The ritual of judgment will boomerang and imperial claims to justice will evaporate, and the emperors will cast a vote against themselves.

Because Koester insisted that New Testament scholars be familiar with Zanker and S. R. F. Price, we can read Justin within the propaganda and amid the images and structures of empire. It is in a context like that of the Forum of Trajan—or more simply, the presence of busts of emperors in courtrooms, or nearly any city square—that Justin and many other early Christians claim to address the emperors while critiquing statuary and its proliferation. In doing so they join their elite pagan colleagues in implicitly criticizing imperial participation in the same, whether this participation came in the form of imperial benefactions that aided in temple building and renovations, or imperial assent to the erection of statues for their own cults or for the cults of their families. Justin argues that the emperors themselves use the sign of the cross even as they erect their own divinized images, not knowing its true meaning.

> The power of this form [the cross] is shown by your own symbols on what are called standards and trophies, to the accompaniment of which all your state procession are made, using these as the signs of your rule and power, even though you do so without knowing. And with this form you set up the images of your deceased emperors, and you name them gods by inscriptions. (*1 Apol.* 55; ET Barnard [1997], 63)

We can imagine the standards and bronze trophies on the Basilica Ulpia in Trajan's Forum—or we can imagine Justin imagining them. Justin theorizes Roman religion in such a way that Roman military triumph and messages of imperial godhood are effectively conducted under the sign of the cross, under the sign of Christianity.

But it's not quite so simple. Justin with his powers of Greek *paideia* isn't really one of the poor who walks the city, although he certainly is subjected to imperial power and both appeals to and resists it in his apologies. Elsewhere Justin offers a critique of statuary typical of near-contemporary and later Christian texts. He accuses the artisan who hammers and planes, cuts and crafts a god—the very sort of gods that Koester shows regularly in slides or on site. Justin elevates the mockery of such cult statues to a new level in his assertion that the artisans are impure. He says coyly, "not to enter into details, [they] are given to all kinds of vice, you very well know; they corrupt even their slave girls who work alongside them. What stupidity, that dissolute people should be said to fashion and make gods for public worship" (Justin *1 Apol.* 9; ET Barnard, 28). Justin uses status markers—the stupidity and pollution of the simple artisan dallying with his low status cohorts—and in doing so appeals to an elite audience. The bodies of female slaves, always expendable, are part of Justin's joke, and we are reminded to consider again the patronage system of the ancient Mediterranean that Koester rejects, and how Christians intersected with it, some walking the city more safely than others.

A day walking a city in ruins closes with a cool glass of piney retsina or raki milky with ice. On a chilly evening in Selçuk, we drink with the archaeologists, and Helmut insists we should all swim the next day at Pamucak. We spill out of the restaurant and from the city center hear the bell-ring of metal against marble as a new sculptor creates a monument for recent war and genocide, even though night has fallen. The church of St. John looks down from its hill at the nearly erased wonder of the world, the ancient Ephesian Temple of Artemis. A modern, kitschy many-breasted Artemis is the patron goddess even of modern Selçuk, looming over a fountain at a busy intersection. In Koester's mind, he is patron to no one, despite having given us all these gifts, and we are clients only of each other. Small and thoughtful among the urban monuments—archaeologists, stray fellow travelers, students who will become each other's trusted conversation partners over the years—we walk the city.

—*Laura Nasrallah*

I WAS A second-year master's student when I first ventured into Harvard's Advanced Seminar for New Testament students or, "Lower Seminar," as it was often called. Helmut Koester was the leader of the seminar that year and the subject was the tools and tasks of exegesis. The organization was simple; each student selected a section of the New Testament and spent the year walking the class through a close examination of that text. Beginning with textual criticism and moving to source, form, redaction criticisms, and beyond, we all became intimately acquainted with our texts and the history of their interpretation. It is obvious to me now that, although I spent a great deal of time with 1 Corinthians 1–4 that year, I learned a whole lot more from Helmut about being a scholar and a teacher.

I remember vividly one day when a student presented on a text-critical problem in her text. The class deliberated for a while—each peering at the cryptic code of the apparatus in their Nestle-Aland 27th edition and puzzling over the various readings. As the group reached consensus, Helmut brought the conversation to a close, decisively annunciating in his staccato German accent: "Ah, yes, well. That settles that." He then took up his blue ballpoint pen and crossed the no-longer-preferred reading from his Greek New Testament. I was struck, and still am, by his willingness to make considered judgments and to change his mind when new arguments are made. For Helmut, what is printed in a book, even in the religious or academic canon, is never the last word on anything.

Helmut teaches his students the value of investigating things for themselves, knowing the primary texts and artifacts and taking their particularity seriously. For Helmut, there is no devil in the details, the peculiar wording, or disjointed argument. Rather, in a close reading of the text or an archaeological site lie its potential, interest, and endless value. Many Harvard students will long remember the short papers that Helmut required us to write each week discussing some aspect of a primary text from the ancient world. He never dictated what we should write, he only asked us to become observant readers and, through this, analytical thinkers.

Taking *all* the primary materials of antiquity seriously has energized Helmut's work with both non-canonical texts and Greco-Roman archaeology. It has always pressed the field of New Testament studies to see the diversity of early Christianity fully within the context of the complex and dynamic social and economic world of the Roman Empire. In 1971, Helmut's path-breaking work with Jim Robinson in *Trajectories through Early Christianity*, called for a re-telling of Christian history through a reassessment of its categories, which too often serve as static backgrounds over and against which to read early Christianity. As a result, the notion of diverse Christianity, and the problematic and constructed nature of such categories as "Hellenism," "Gnosticism," or "heresy," have become critical commonplaces in the work of his students and, more broadly, in the scholarly conversation of New Testament studies as a whole.

For me, Helmut's contributions range fully from the historical to the hermeneutical. Over the years at Harvard I came to know that there were many corrections, emendations, and deletions in his Nestle-Aland Greek New Testament. After a while, when I was his teaching fellow, I would smile knowingly when the Introduction to the New Testament students shifted with discomfort when Helmut would direct them to cross some phrase out of their Bibles. Once he even instructed them to tear the book of Jude from their Bibles for its lack of scholarly interest and theological value. I could tell the students did not know if they should laugh or dutifully tear it out. For me the message was clear—we are the keepers and interpreters of the Christian tradition. We interrogate it, analyze it, evaluate it, and explicate it. It is not the keeper of us, neither of our minds nor our commitments.

Although it does not always take me in similar directions, Helmut's view that biblical interpretation and historical criticism *matter* has had a profound impact on me. In *Trajectories*, Robinson and Koester offered their essays as experiments that sought to "open up new perspectives both for understanding early Christian history and for perceiving the present problems of Christianity:"

> We have tried to avoid the pitfalls of "disinterested" research, for
> we have sensed the danger of merely playing in the sandbox of

irrelevant scholarship. We want to be taught by history, not in order to find our own position reaffirmed, but in order to be exposed to and to learn from the complex and agonizing decisions [of history]. (269)

They suggested that the ways in which Christian communities have translated and continue to translate the historical particularity of Jesus into different cultural contexts is a hermeneutical problem common to the historian, the theologian, and the interpreter. In my view, identifying, describing, analyzing, and evaluating these instantiations is one of the ways biblical scholars participate in contemporary religious and political debates. Twenty years after *Trajectories*, Koester expresses this in a way that resonates with me: "Interpretation of the Bible is justified only if it is a source for political and religious renewal, or it is not worth the effort. . . . If the Bible has anything to do with justice and freedom, biblical scholarship must be able to question those very structures of power and expose their injustice and destructive potential" (*The Future of Early Christianity*, 475).

The way that investigating history helps us take a critical look at our own contexts becomes quite apparent to me whenever I travel with students to Greece and Turkey—one of my most Koesterian traditions. For example, in January 2003, I traveled with fifteen Luther College students to Greece and Turkey to study the historical and social context of early Christianity. We tromped around the rocks in Athens, Philippi, and Pergamon, puzzling over this foundation or that inscription. Near the end of our three-week trip, we sat at the top of the enormous theater in the city of Ephesos looking out on the Harbor Street and imagining the bustling ancient waterfront. At one point, a member of our group decided to test the acoustics in the theater, descending to the orchestra and reading aloud the story of the riot of the Ephesian silversmiths in Acts 19:23-41. Arriving at verse 34, she called out the crowd's words, "Great is Artemis of the Ephesians!" Energized by the resounding chant and by all that they had learned about the history and iconography of the Ephesian Artemis, many members of the class returned the shout: "Great is Artemis of the Ephesians!" I was mortified. "Tourists," I thought. However, the moment

was not a pedagogical lost cause. Shortly after my students' brazen shout-
ing, a large group of Korean tourists came into the theater near the stage.
They had just arrived on a large cruise ship at the port of Kusadası. As
we watched, four men from the group ceremoniously took center stage
and, with great energy and in their best English, began to sing a chorus
of "How Great Thou Art."

We applauded. And then we had a discussion about religious tour-
ism, economics, and empire—after all, they were Midwestern Lutheran
college students listening to Korean Presbyterians touring Turkey singing a German hymn, in English. We talked about how the story in Acts
trades on the notion that the new Christian communities represented
an economic threat to the artisans of Ephesus who made silver statues
for visitors to the temple of the Ephesian Artemis. There are still religious tourists coming to Ephesus. The gods have changed but the realities of economics and politics have not. We thought about the nearby
façade with all the gods of the empire and the Temple of the Flavian
Sebastoi looming above it. We talked about how today the gods are lined
up beneath the god of capitalism. After all, you can buy both little silver
Artemises and miniature silver Christian icons at the same shops, run by
Turkish Muslims, along the side of the road in Selçuk.

This kind of conversation—with a community of learners analyzing,
theorizing, and making connections to contemporary realities—typifies
my own experience as Helmut's student. While it surprised me on that
day in Advanced NT seminar, the fact that a conversation with a group of
students could settle an issue for Helmut is the rule not the exception. He
treats students like colleagues and friends. It was around the table in our
doctoral seminars and at the local Chinese restaurant that I learned that
good intellectual work happens in community. Helmut has always gathered his students together for meals and conversation both in Cambridge
and in Greece and Turkey. He has always brought people together to
learn from each other's work and thus embodies a pedagogy not based
on status and top-down academic hierarchies, but on collegiality and the
view that it is in the exchange of ideas, values, and talents that real learning happens. This is the kind of collegiality, respect for students, and love

of the intellectual life that characterizes Helmut Koester. I am grateful to Helmut for such a legacy and I aspire to carry it forward.

—*Melanie Johnson-Debaufre*

I T IS not an exaggeration to say that Helmut Koester changed my life: I moved from the Netherlands to the United States to study with him. I first met Helmut when he was a visiting professor at the Vrije Universiteit in Amsterdam in the Fall of 1992. Helmut taught a course on the archaeology of the New Testament world—my first of many more that I enjoyed. Three times I had the privilege to travel through Greece and Turkey with Helmut, David Mitten, and Mimi Bonz. These trips were fantastic, mind-opening experiences that have made the world of antiquity, that in which the early Christians lived, come alive for me.

The apse mosaic in the small, fifth-century church of Hosios David, high up near the ancient city wall in Thessaloniki, depicts a young, beardless Christ seated on a rainbow. From a corner of Helmut's office, this Christ gazes at you. This stunningly beautiful mosaic, to which Helmut has taken so many of his students, symbolizes for me in a variety of ways much of what Helmut stands for and has taught me.

To look at this picture yourselves, to conjure up that office and those long, generous meetings with Helmut, you need only go online to the "Visual Information Access" of Harvard University Libraries. The fact that Helmut digitized his important collection of slides, making it available to all on the World Wide Web, is another of his great contributions to scholarship of the world of early Christianity and a sign of his firm belief in democracy and in teaching.

In the Thessalonican apse mosaic, the central image is that of Christ surrounded by representations of the four evangelists holding their books. Central in Helmut's work is his groundbreaking research on early Christian gospels; from his early work on the gospel quotations in Justin Martyr, to his work on the Gospel of Thomas, the Dialogue of the Savior and the canonical gospels.

The apse mosaic is rich with biblical allusions; it embodies the principle of Helmut's teaching that the visual and the literary come together and that students must take both seriously in order to gain a deep understanding of the ancient world. Books take a prominent place in the mosaic; besides the codices of the four evangelists, two scrolls with inscriptions are depicted. Christ holds a scroll that reads:

> Behold our God, for whom we hope,
> and we rejoiced in our salvation,
> that he may give rest to this house.

With this text, a paraphrase of Isaiah 25:9-10a (LXX), the mosaicist indicates that this is a theophany. Thus the words in the inscription support the interpretation of the portrait of Christ on the throne.

But there is more to this than gospels and books: the Christ-figure in the mosaic is depicted against a background of city and mountains. This earthly background represents Christ's presence in everyday life. This coordinates with the actualizing paraphrase of the biblical text. The prophet Isaiah described a vision of God's comforting presence. For the fifth-century mosaicist, however, this theophany is not a promise for the future but rather a representation of Christ's real presence in the lives of believers gathering in this house of worship. This interpretation of the mosaic resonates with Helmut's wider understanding of early Christian eschatology as a realized eschatology in conversation with similar Roman claims to kingship and peace.

The immediate context of the Isaiah passage is the vision of the banquet on the mountain with rich food and well-aged wine. I think of the many meals Helmut has shared with his students—from lavish Thanksgiving feasts in Lexington in the company of international scholars and friends, to weekly dinner gatherings after class with teaching fellows in a Chinese restaurant in Cambridge, to sharing food and retsina in many restaurants in Greece and Turkey, and family dinners with Helmut and Gisela, my husband Jan Willem and my parents, when the latter were visiting us from the Netherlands.

Helmut's fine scholarship and his infectious love for the texts and material world of early Christianity have greatly influenced my scholarship and teaching. I am grateful for this great gift and will do my best to follow his example.

—AnneMarie Luijendijk

Afterword

Klaus Baltzer

It was 1954 when I came to Heidelberg to work with Gerhard von Rad as his *Assistent* in Old Testament. Helmut Koester was *Privatdozent* and *Assistent* to Günther Bornkamm in New Testament. We were allotted one workroom together in the *Akademie der Wissenschaften*. We greeted each other quite formally: "Herr Köster"—"Herr Balzter." It was more polite than the military experience we both had endured. We had both witnessed the end of the war with its collapse. We had not ever been victorious. Helmut was there at the bombing of Helgoland, I was with the army that ended up encircled in the Ruhr. Death and dying came close to us. That was also true for our friend Dieter Georgi (died March 2005), who witnessed the destruction of Dresden. These experiences form the background for the arrival of peace and justice.

There was no way for us to avoid discussing 'Bible' from the standpoint of both the Old and of the New Testament. One example was the notice of Hegesippus, transmitted through Justin, that James the brother of the Lord had the nickname "Oblias," with a scriptural allusion to Obadiah 1, "fortress for the nations." After eager searching through Mandelkern (the Hebrew concordance) and Hatch & Redpath (the Greek Septuagint concordance) from front to back we determined that there had been a scribal error. Instead of "Oblias" the reading should have been "Obdias," with the delta losing its horizontal line to look just like a lambda. The outcome was a Note in the *ZNW*, our very first publication and still of interest to us today ("Die Bezeichnung des Jakobus als OBLIAS," *ZNW* 46 [1955] 141–42). Did James have the nickname "Servant of God"?

When our wives arrived on the scene, the formality was gone. My Jo was a singer, played the violin, Gisela accompanied masterfully on the piano. Choral singing also played a part. After our children were born at roughly the same time, we went on Sundays to university worship services at the Peterskirche, which most of the professors of the theol-

139

ogy faculty attended. Together we would take long nature walks on the *Königstuhl* and in the *Oberwald*. Some ladies commented "It's really unusual to have these scholarly gentlemen pushing a baby carriage around the University!" (Such were the times!) We have continued till today with similar hiking trips. In our scholarly work, besides collaborating in the main seminars of the professors, we ran the *Proseminars*. These had up to forty participants, so one had to share the work. Every student had to write a major paper. That was our apprenticeship.

But in addition to this we had already begun an interdisciplinary conference on exegesis together with the *Assistent* in practical theology, our friend Friedemann Merkel. That was the start of the "Exegetical-Homiletical Working Group." Since Helmut had done his Habilitation by then, he could convene it for us officially. We wrote exegeses and meditations for the *Göttinger Predigtmeditationen* (*GPM*) on the lectionary readings of the church year. They are some of the best exegetical works that we have ever published. All three of us had experienced as pastors how much the Gospel could be diluted for congregations. Our intention was that the Theology Faculty should serve people in the community and the church no differently than would Medicine and Law.

The Heidelberg Faculty and University offered excellent opportunities at this time for scholarly exchange among the different subjects. It was a time noted for breakthroughs. We knew from our teachers, Rudolf Bultmann and Günther Bornkamm as well as Gerhard von Rad and Martin Noth, that they had professed their Christian faith during the Third Reich boldly and deliberately. We never heard anti-Semitic expressions from them. The biblical tradition was attended to in its fullness and its entirety. There was strong interest in the history of traditions. The continuity as well as the difference between Old and New Testament was noticed. There was no question for our teachers whether the message of the Bible applied to Jews as much as to Christians. The connection to Islam was not yet a topic of interest.

We were persuaded by the essays of our teachers in historical-critical research, but we saw the necessity of taking apart and reconstituting the key terms *Vorverständnis, Gattung, Sitz im Leben, Tradition, Geschichte,* and *Heilsgeschichte,* in brief: to develop hermeneutics further.

There was of course a break in our connection when Helmut received the call to Harvard in 1958. When we parted we told each other "Let's stay in touch." This we have done.

The contributions to this volume give an excellent picture of the time that followed, the beginnings at Harvard and afterwards, so I can limit myself to a couple of points. As for Helmut and me, scarcely a year has passed in which we haven't met. The publishing house Fortress Press played a big part in making this possible. In 1963—when I had become a professor for the first time, namely at the Garrett Biblical Institute—Helmut knocked on the door of our house in Evanston and said, "We are founding a commentary series!" That was (along with Frank Moore Cross and James M. Robinson) the beginning of *Hermeneia*. The goal was to bring the most diverse exegetical traditions together by means of commentaries and thus also to pay close attention to texts from the broader context of the Bible. The commentaries were supposed to be accessible to "interested people." Over the years Helmut's organizational ability, his diligence (including with the proofs), his encouragement, and his critical sense were most impressive.

Helmut entered a "New World" in the literal sense with his excursions to Greece and Turkey. This grew out of personal interest—not that the point was to seek "the footprints of Jesus in the sand." The physical context is needed to understand the Bible. Texts, geographical data, archaeological artifacts must all be correlated. The stones do not speak. We discovered that the more familiar we became with antiquity, the more closely it drew us in.

We have not conducted our research *about* these countries, but *with* the colleagues living there. Thus a network of scholarly connections and confidence has developed, often with quite personal input from Helmut. Archives and storerooms became accessible. Nearly always we were led on site by the excavators or had their letters of reference to open doors. Another aspect not to be forgotten is the local innkeepers in the places we went. You had to be there to appreciate the warmth. We became true guests, whether in Thasos, Santorini, Corinth, or Herakleia. We were brought up to date on what had happened since Helmut's last visit and what was new—including in archaeology.

I have participated in four of these trips. Helmut gave me the task of paying special attention to connections with Egypt, Mesopotamia, in short to the so-called "Near East" (what Egyptologist ever wanders into the museum of a small city in Greece or Turkey?). Right there some fairly interdisciplinary work was being done. We were particularly interested (and grew more so the further we went) in the special function of sanctuaries, places of pilgrimage, and oracular sites with their connections, economic ties, the roads built for military purposes on which merchants and ideas traveled, in sum the system of cities.

When Helmut invited me on a seminar trip for the first time, he said, "Now you, just like all the rest, will have to make a report and take the lead when we visit a site." He assigned Aigina to me, since the Aiginetan sculptures were on exhibit at the Glyptothek in Munich. I am still interested in and working on Aigina.

Seldom have I learned so much as with the evening reports on the trips that introduced us to what we would see the next day. Where else had I ever spent time surrounded by so many experts in various fields as with these graduate students—ranging from prehistory, the Old Testament, New Testament, church history, right down to Byzantine studies. They were always "Upper Seminars." And what site guides! David Mitten helped us translate bilingual inscriptions (the basis for understanding the Septuagint), Klaus Nohlen and his people helped us understand the architecture ("So how old would these walls be?").

One result of these repeated trips is that we found out how problematic staying inside one's comfort zone is for scholarship. All too easily everybody keeps to his nice little field set apart. The temporal and geographic connections are there to see. We must practice a sound method that acknowledges our own role in the story.

Another thing that binds me to Helmut is the timespan of our interests. I start with the Persian period, to which Deutero-Isaiah (Isaiah 40–55) belongs, and go down to Alexander, known to the Book of Daniel. Helmut begins his *Introduction* with Alexander and ends with Constantine (therefore not Droysen's historical plan "From Alexander to Augustus"). Helmut can still debate productively and let himself be convinced.

One cannot reach eighty years of age without having some painful experiences as well—in the University as in the Church. So it was a good experience for Helmut Koester to have the honorary doctorate conferred on him by Humboldt University in 2006. The bestowal of the degree took place in the Berlin Cathedral, where the Protestant Theology Faculty is located, in the presence of the Rektor of the University, Christoph Markschies, and the Bishop of Berlin, Wolfgang Huber.

What especially ties me to Helmut today is the legacy we pass on to the next generation. Here, too, Helmut has contributed so much already. What counts is not just the results of the work, but above all the questions we choose to grapple with. They are what's most valuable! This volume testifies to that.

—*Klaus Baltzer*

Helmut and Gisela in Turkey

Notes on Contributors

Ellen Bradshaw Aitken

Th.D. 1997
Dissertation: "The Morphology of the Passion Narrative"
Associate Professor of Early Christian History and Literature
McGill University

Harold W. Attridge

Ph.D. 1975
Dissertation: "The Presentation of Biblical History
   in the Antiquitates Judaicae of Flavius Josephus"
Lillian Claus Professor of New Testament and Dean
Yale Divinity School

Klaus Baltzer

Professor Emeritus of Old Testament
University of Munich

Arthur Bellinzoni

Ph.D. 1962
Dissertation: "The Sayings of Jesus in the Writings of Justin Martyr"
Professor of Religion Emeritus
Wells College

Gary A. Bisbee

Th.D. 1986
Dissertation: "Pre-Decian Acts of Martyrs and Commentarii"
Self-Employed Publications Typesetter, Pepperel, MA

Ann Graham Brock

Ph.D. 2000
Dissertation: "Authority, Politics, and Gender in Early Christianity:
    Mary, Peter, and the Portrayal of Leadership"
Adjunct Faculty
Iliff School of Theology

John Clabeaux

Ph.D. 1983
Dissertation: "The Pauline Corpus which Marcion Used:
    The Text of the Letters of Paul in the Early Second Century"
Assistant Professor of Scripture and Biblical Languages
Pontifical College Josephinum

Eldon Jay Epp

Ph.D. 1961
Dissertation: "Theological Tendency in the Textual Variants of
    Codex Bezae Cantabrigiensis: Anti-Judaic Tendencies in Acts"
Harkness Professor of Biblical Literature Emeritus
Case Western Reserve University

Everett Ferguson

Ph.D. 1959
Dissertation: "Ordination in the Ancient Church:
    An Examination of the Theological and Constitutional
    Motifs in the Light of Biblical and Gentile Sources"
Professor of Bible Emeritus and Distinguished Scholar-in-Residence
Abilene Christian University

Steven J. Friesen

Ph.D. 1990
Dissertation: "Ephesos: Twice Neokoros"
Louise Farmer Boyer Professor in Biblical Studies
University of Texas, Austin

Melanie Johnson-DeBaufre

Th.D. 2002
Dissertation: "It's the End of the World as We Know It:
   Eschatology, Q, and the Construction of Christian Origins"
Assistant Professor of New Testament and Early Christianity
Drew University Theological School

Robert A. Kraft

Ph.D. 1961
Dissertation: "The Epistle of Barnabas: Its Quotations and Their Sources"
Berg Professor of Religious Studies Emeritus
University of Pennsylvania

AnneMarie Luijendijk

Th.D. 2005
Dissertation: "Fragments from Oxyrhynchus:
   A Case Study in Early Christian Identity"
Assistant Professor of Religion
Princeton University

Dennis MacDonald

Ph.D. 1978
Dissertation: "There Is No Male and Female:
   Galatians 3:26-28 and Gnostic Baptismal Tradition"
Professor of Religion
Claremont Graduate University

Jennifer K. Berenson Maclean

Ph.D. 1995
Dissertation: "Ephesians and the Problem of Colossians:
   Interpretation of Texts and Traditions in Eph 1:1-2:10"
Associate Professor of Religion
Roanoke College

Notes on Contributors

Christopher R. Matthews

Th.D. 1993
Dissertation: "Trajectories through the Philip Tradition"
Editor of *New Testament Abstracts* and
Adjunct Associate Professor of New Testament
Weston Jesuit School of Theology

Shelly Matthews

Th.D. 1997
Dissertation: "High Standing Women and Mission and Conversion:
    A Rhetorical-Historical Analysis of the *Antiquities* and Acts"
Associate Professor of Religion
Furman University

Lee Martin McDonald

Th.M. 1985
Thesis: "An Examination of the Origins of the Christian Canon"
President and Professor of Biblical Studies, Acadia Divinity College
Dean of the Faculty of Theology, Acadia University

Laura Nasrallah

Th.D. 2002
Dissertation: "'An Ecstasy of Folly':
Rhetorical Strategies in Early Christian Debates over Prophecy"
Assistant Professor of New Testament
Harvard Divinity School

George W. E. Nickelsburg

Th.D. 1968
Dissertation: "Resurrection, Immortality,
    and Eternal Life in Intertestamental Judaism"
Professor of Religion Emeritus
University of Iowa

Michael O'Laughlin

Th.D. 1987
Dissertation: "Origenism in the Desert:
   Anthropology and Integration in Evagrius Ponticus"
Spiritual director, Healing Center
Arlington, Massachusetts

Carolyn Osiek

Th.D. 1978
Dissertation: "Rich and Poor in the Shepherd of Hermas"
Charles Fisher Catholic Professor of New Testament
Brite Divinity School

Elaine Pagels

Ph.D. 1970
Dissertation: "The Hermeneutical Debate between Origen and
   Heracleon in Origen's Commentary on the Gospel of John"
Harrington Spear Paine Foundation Professor of Religion
Princeton University

Stephen J. Patterson

M.T.S. 1983
Ph.D. 1988, Claremont Graduate School
Professor of New Testament
Eden Theological Seminary

Birger A. Pearson

Ph.D. 1968
Dissertation: "The Pneumatikos-Psychikos Terminology in 1 Corinthians:
   A Study in the Theology of the Opponents of Paul
   and Its Relation to Gnosticism"
Professor of Religious Studies Emeritus
University of California, Santa Barbara

Richard I. Pervo

Th.D. 1979
Dissertation: "The Literary Genre of the Acts of the Apostles"
Formerly Professor of New Testament and Patristics
Seabury-Western Theological Seminary

Norman R. Petersen

Ph.D. 1967
Dissertation: "The Literary Problematic of the Apocryphon of John"
Washington Gladden Professor of Religion Emeritus
Williams College

David M. Scholer

Th.D. 1980
Dissertation: "Israel Murdered Its Prophets: The Origins and
    Development of the Tradition in the Old Testament and Judaism"
Associate Dean for the Center for Advanced Theological Studies
    and Professor of New Testament
Fuller Theological Seminary

Daniel Schowalter

Th.D. 1989
Dissertation: "The Relationship between the Emperor and the Gods:
    Images from Pliny's *Panegyricus* and Other Sources from the Time of Trajan"
Professor of Religion and Classics
Carthage College

Philip Sellew

Th.D. 1986
Dissertation: "Early Collections of Jesus' Words:
    The Development of Dominical Discourses"
Associate Professor of Classical and Near Eastern Studies
University of Minnesota

Dennis E. Smith

Th.D. 1980
Dissertation: "Social Obligation in the Context of Communal Meals:
   A Study of the Christian Meal in 1 Corinthians in
   Comparison with Graeco-Roman Communal Meals"
Professor of New Testament
Phillips Theological Seminary

James D. Smith III

Th.D. 1986
Dissertation: "The Ignatian Long Recension and
   Christian Communities in Fourth Century Syrian Antioch"
Associate Professor of Church History, Bethel Seminary San Diego
Lecturer in Theology and Religious Studies, University of San Diego

Krister Stendahl

Professor of Divinity Emeritus, Harvard Divinity School
Formerly Archbishop of Stockholm

Robert F. Stoops, Jr.

Ph.D. 1983
Dissertation: "Miracle Stories and Vision Reports in the *Acts of Peter*"
Professor of Religion
Western Washington University

Christine M. Thomas

Ph.D. 1995
"The *Acts of Peter*, the Ancient Novel, and Early Christian History"
Associate Professor of Religious Studies
University of California, Santa Barbara

David L. Tiede

Ph.D. 1970
Dissertation: "The Charismatic Figure as Miracle Worker"
Bernhard M. Christensen Professor of Religion and Vocation, Augsburg College
Professor of New Testament and President Emeritus, Luther Seminary

Notes on Contributors

Demetrios (Trakatellis)

Ph.D. 1971
Dissertation: "The Pre-existence of Christ in the Writings of Justin Martyr: An
 Exegetical Study with Reference to the
 Humiliation and Exaltation Christology"
Archbishop of America, Greek Orthodox Archdiocese of America

James C. Walters

Ph.D. Boston University, 1991
Dissertation: "Ethnic Issues in Paul's Letter to the Romans:
 Changing Self-Definitions in Earliest Roman Christianity."
Associate Professor of New Testament
Boston University School of Theology

Demetrius K. Williams

Ph.D. 1997
Dissertation: "'Enemies of the Cross of Christ': A Rhetorical Analysis of the
 'Theology of the Cross' in Conflict in Paul's Philippian Correspondence"
Associate Professor of New Testament, Tulane University, 1996–2005
Visiting Professor of New Testament, Central Baptist Theological Seminary